"Leslie Reyes shares deeply personal stories of trauma and triumph in this wise and inspiring guide to grabbing the handlebars of life and steering it exactly where you want to go."

—Jen Sincero, *New York Times* Bestselling Author of *You Are a Badass*

"I first 'met' Leslie (actually, just now realized we've only ever met virtually) when I made a shout out on the internet looking for inspirational, modern women in motorcycles to feature in a calendar for 2022. Her story of overcoming mental illness, that of her own and of family members, and the aftermath and anxiety that can come after it, is truly inspirational. She found herself in a place where she wasn't who she wanted to be, couldn't do what she wanted to do, so she placed herself in a situation where she would be harshly tested so that she could overcome it: she decided to learn to ride motorcycles. Her journey learning to ride is one of the most challenging I've heard yet, with her past demons creating such deep existing anxiety that was fully exposed in such a challenging sport. You'll be hooked into her story with just the first page. Hers is a relatable, beautiful story of how much more can happen when, instead of just settling or drugging your problems away to a quiet submission, you go through the darkness and never give up until you've overcome them."

—Carolyn, aka "Doodle on a Motorcycle", YouTube Motovlogger

"The Zen of Learning to Ride a Motorcycle is really a manual on how to live in this world. Leslie Reyes' confrontation with one of her greatest fears, riding a motorcycle, made her aware of ten essential practices or habits that she needed to develop in order to overcome blocks to safely ride a motorcycle. In the process, she realized that by not having developed these habits much earlier in her life, she continued to replicate and repeat self-destructive patterns over and over in relationships, jobs, and when making important decisions. While this book at times feels like a joyride into the past, Leslie quickly takes you to the edge of a cliff. You will feel joy, laughter, sadness, heart-break, and triumph when you read about her experiences. You will spot aspects of yourself in this book, and hopefully it will trigger the vulnerability that it takes to heal as Leslie has shown us."

—Regina Petterson, Psy.D., Clinical Psychologist

"The Zen of Learning to Ride a Motorcycle drew me in with Leslie's authentic sharing of her life – both the devastating times and the triumphant. I felt I was in the room with her, either on the verge of tears, attempting to whisper advice, or fist pumping to cheer her on! This book is WAY more than motorcycles! The way she weaves her Zen Motorcycle Habits with her life lessons is genius and paves a path of empathy to those we meet every day with no concept of the struggles they may be facing or what they've overcome. Read this book if you want to be inspired by Leslie's demonstration of the human spirit's will to pursue healing, epic love, and adventure."

—Jen Burch, Hightail Hair Founder

"Leslie's engaging storytelling voice had me hooked on *The Zen of Learning to Ride a Motorcycle* from the first sentence. She has a unique way of weaving the stories of her colorful life together with the lessons she's learned on her motorcycle. Leslie's life story is at once entertaining, fascinating, heart-breaking, and ultimately hopeful and inspiring. This is a must read for anyone who has struggled with trauma, mental health challenges, and any of the myriad stresses we all endure in life."

—Jennifer Hondru, Reiki Master, Yoga Teacher, and Mindfulness Teacher

"A good memoir is above all, honest. Leslie Reyes' *The Zen of Learning to Ride a Motorcycle* delivers a no-holds-bar exploration of one woman's experience of dealing with and healing from the residual trauma of having a schizophrenic parent. Using the metaphor of learning to ride a motorcycle, the author applies the lessons she gathers from the struggles and triumphs in becoming a bona-fide biker, to the adult pit falls she faced having grown up as a girl in chaos. You don't need a motor-cycle to appreciate the journey, and you don't need to have first-hand knowledge of a serious mental-illness. The lessons here are laid out in plain language, and the ride is a thrill."

—Tawny Sverdlin, MLIS

"Honestly, this book is amazing. I laughed out-loud, I felt empowered, and I cried. I find myself thinking of the ten Zen principles outlined in this story from time to time, and I continue to learn from them. Really. This is a powerful book."

—Sherri Todd, BSN, RNC-NIC, NICU Nurse

"Reyes presents an honest and well thought-out perspective of the insight she has gained through the Zen of motorcycle riding. This is an essential read for any level of rider, or anyone who hasn't championed a skill or lifelong dream, no matter the reason. The Motorcycle is the hook and reel, but the way Reyes presents her true and honest worldview makes you appreciate this book no matter who the reader. It deserves applause for a job well-done."

—Tabitha Fielteau, Chic Riot Co-Founder, Moto fashion gear brand

"*The Zen of Learning to Ride a Motorcycle* is a phenomenal and intimate journey through a life story that I feel like I could have written parts of myself. Not only does Reyes spend time on the tragedies that deeply affected her life, she also explains and lays out how to find Zen in various real-life situations. An uplifting, sometimes gasp-worthy, journey through her life, I highly recommend this to anyone who has dealt with mental illness in their family, within themselves, or anyone who enjoys an amazing story about how understanding Zen truly changed this motorcyclist's life. Her stories reminded me to keep working at it but still respect myself and overcome hurdles at my own pace. 'How you do one thing is how you do everything' is one of my favorite themes throughout this book. I try to focus on that quote and improve myself every day after reading this incredibly inspirational story!"

—Brittany Williams, Voice-Over Artist and Actress

"I love the way this is written like an owner's manual for your life!"

—Jaqueline Patterson, Human Rights Activist and Patient Advocate

THE ZEN OF LEARNING TO RIDE A MOTORCYCLE

THE ZEN OF LEARNING TO RIDE A MOTORCYCLE

HOW I FACED MY FEARS, SHIFTED GEARS, AND
FOUND HEALING FROM ANXIETY,
CODEPENDENCY, AND DEPRESSION

LESLIE REYES

LOLA66 PUBLISHING

The Zen of Learning to Ride a Motorcycle: How I Faced My Fears, Shifted Gears, and Found Healing from Anxiety, Codependency, and Depression

ISBN: 979-8-9855703-0-4 (Paperback)
ISBN: 979-8-9855703-1-1 (ePub)

Library of Congress Control Number: 2022905965

Edited by Brooks Becker
Interior design by Jenny Lisk
Cover design by Valentina G. at 99Designs

Lyrics to "What it Seems" by Leslie Reyes and the band Mama, © 2001

Published by Lola66 Publishing, Los Angeles, California

For Sherri

CONTENTS

FOREWORD

ALICE O'LEARY RANDALL

Here's a confession: you can probably count on one hand the number of times I have been on a motorcycle, and I have never driven one. Another confession: I'm not really big on self-help books. So, why am I writing the foreword to *The Zen of Learning to Ride a Motorcycle: How I Faced My Fears, Shifted Gears, and Found Healing from Anxiety, Codependency, and Depression?* Because I *am* really big on writing, any kind of writing—essays, books, letters, diaries, blogs, even letters to the editor. My father taught me the value of writing and how writing can become almost a friend. It can change how a person thinks and acts. Heck, it can change the world.

And that is another thing I am big about—change. It is the only constant in life. And while some changes are bigger than others, the simple fact is that learning how, in the immortal words REO Speedwagon, to "Roll with the Changes," is a critical component of life. We all must find the tools to help us through the changes, and it seems to me that Leslie has done just that.

From the moment I first met Leslie in 2014, it was clear to me she was going through some big changes. Our meet-ups were confined to medical cannabis conferences and at each one I would learn a bit more about Leslie. At one conference Leslie rather casually dropped the fact that her mother was schizophrenic. Her honesty in that moment made me respect her more than I already did, and it also helped explain a restlessness I felt from her.

In between conferences we kept up with one another's activities on Facebook. It was here that I learned of her permanent move to California. Her love of the state was evident, but for a while she was torn between California and her home state of New Jersey. It was clear that she was happier in the Golden State and when you find your geographic place it can change everything. Leslie's husband joined her in Southern California, and there were dogs, beach walks, and fun. I watched her blossom on Facebook.

And now she has written a book that weaves her life experience with the Ten Principles of Good Motorcycle Riding Habits. Finding a passion in life that also lends itself to Life Guidance is truly a gift. For me that passion was golf, for some it can be painting, or hiking, or sailing and on and on. Leslie seems to have found her Life Guidance passion in motorcycle riding.

The title of this book is a play on the 1974 book by Robert Pirsig, *Zen and the Art of Motorcycle Maintenance*, which, in turn, was a play on a 1948 book *Zen and the Art of Archery* by Eugen Herrigel. It was Herrigel, a German philosopher, who introduced the concept of Zen to parts of Europe. Alas, his love of Zen was not enough to keep him from making a very bad life decision when he chose to support the Nazis. It seems that Herr Herrigel might have missed the part about using Zen to understand the meaning of life without being misled by logical thought or language, not to mention the Zen practice of removing prejudices.

Leslie's embrace of Zen, as it applies to her new love of motorcycle riding, seems more true to the philosophy's original goal. Applying the ten tenets of motorcycle riding to events in her life has allowed her to view these events from a different point of view without assumptions, prejudices, or expectations. It is an enviable accomplishment.

Alice O'Leary Randall
July 2021

PREFACE

Let's address the elephant in the Room. Why did I name my book "The Zen of Learning to Ride a Motorcycle" when there is a famous book already out there called "Zen and the Art of Motorcycle Maintenance" by Robert Pirsig?

When I first became inspired to write this book, it was because I had finally learned the concept of "How a person does one thing, is how a person does everything" in the process of learning to ride.

So, initially, I was thinking of names like "Everything I ever needed to learn in life, I learned from my motorcycle" or "How I do motorcycles is how I do life."

But, when I learned that the concept of "How a person does one thing is how a person does everything" actually originated in Zen Buddhism, I knew I had my title.

Mr. Pirsig's book is nearly fifty years old, and I was only four years old when his book was released. His book is written from the male perspective. Very few women were riding motorcycles in 1974, when his book was released. And while today, only 20 percent of motorcycle riders are women, in 1974, only half that many women were riding. I have paid homage to Robert Pirsig in my book, and I hope I've done the name justice. It was not through yoga, astrology, or any other spiritual endeavor that I found Zen. I never imagined my motorcycle would be the guru I needed to find peace of mind in all areas of my life.

This is a true story. The events and dialogue in this book have been recreated to the best of my memory. While some of the names, timeframes, and small details have been changed to protect the privacy of those who I'm no longer in contact with, most of the names of real people were used with their permission. A few events and characters have been consolidated for storytelling purposes.

Some may not remember the events this way, but this is my story taken from my life experiences, and the events are described from my point of view. By writing these stories down, I have found healing from many of the events in my life that had previously scarred me and were either burned into my memory or shoved down so far I had never processed them.

This is the story of how I crawled my way out of the dark and learned to trust myself.

Leslie Reyes, BSN, RN

INTRODUCTION
WHAT IS ZEN?

"How a person does one thing, is how a person does everything."

—ZEN PHILOSOPHY

When I was ten years old, I stopped my schizophrenic mother from committing suicide. Shortly after that, I began having anxiety and panic attacks that were so debilitating I was hospitalized twice. The anxiety interfered with my ability to make any decisions in life on my own well into my thirties and forties. I never learned to trust myself, even after becoming a psychiatric nurse.

My parents were both loving, sweet people who did the best they could with what was in front of them. I didn't realize until much later in life, but my mother's illness had distracted my parents from teaching me certain tools I needed to survive. I was also suffering from an autism spectrum disorder that wasn't diagnosed until I was in my fifties.

Motorcycle riding was a tradition on my Filipino father's side of the family, and kids I grew up with in my neighborhood were always riding around on mini-bikes and mopeds. We must have been about six years old when my neighborhood friend and classmate, Marcus, took me for a ride on his shiny red mini-bike. But as I grew older, I was missing out. I was having panic attacks that were causing me to miss out on more than just learning to ride a motorcycle.

During one particularly difficult time in my life, a therapist recommended I ask my doctor to prescribe me an antidepressant. Unfortunately, my primary care physician prescribed the wrong type of antidepressant for my condition. The medication created symptoms that mimicked bipolar disorder, and I was later misdiagnosed and overmedicated. Being misdiagnosed created yet another barrier to overcoming my struggles with anxiety, depression, panic attacks, insomnia, poor money habits, and codependency into my thirties and forties.

My real addiction was codependency.

I didn't trust myself to do things on my own. Maybe it was because of the culture I was raised in. I believed that if I wanted to pursue my dreams, I needed a partner to help me navigate the scary world around me. Hoping someone else would teach me to have the faith in myself that I lacked, I attached myself to all these relationships. I didn't have enough confidence on my own. In order to live my life, I felt like I had to ask for permission to be me.

We hear it all the time, that we can't be happy in a relationship or find the right relationship, if we haven't learned to feel fulfilled and happy by ourselves first. In the 1970s and 1980s, no one ever really taught girls how to do that.

How do you create the best relationship with yourself?

I never thought a motorcycle would become the guru I needed in order to change my life habits, and learn to trust myself.

The Zen of Learning to Ride a Motorcycle started with one bad habit that I wanted to change.

My motorcycle and I kept ending up on the ground. That's because I was in the habit of slamming on my brakes on my motorcycle and in my car. Both my father and my husband complained about it whenever they were in the car with me.

"You need to plan ahead," my father would say. Meanwhile, my husband would slam on an invisible brake from the passenger's seat.

"You go through too many brake pads."

It was just a bad habit.

When I learned to ride a motorcycle, I brought that bad habit with me. I slammed on the brakes on the motorcycle when I was trying to stop.

I accidentally hit the throttle because I was grabbing the front brake too hard. The motorcycle felt unsteady. I'm short and can only get one foot down. So I instinctively grabbed "the handle bar," which is actually the throttle. My electric motorcycle does not have any gears. So as soon as I hit the throttle, the bike took off.

It happened so fast, I did it three times before I realized I was unintentionally hitting the throttle. I hit the ground violently every time. And every time I did it, I was shaken. Terrified. I'd have to push through the fear to get back on the bike.

So I started changing the way I was driving my car. I wanted to get in the habit of responding to situations in traffic, instead of reacting to them. I wanted to be more mindful, to stop "zoning out" when I was driving my car.

To develop better habits ON the motorcycle, I wanted to start practicing better habits OFF the motorcycle. It didn't take long for me to notice that these small habits were making changes in other areas of my life.

The Ten Zen Principles of Good Motorcycle Riding Habits

1. Respond to situations, instead of reacting.
2. Understand and respect your limitations, and go at your own pace.

3. Be prepared, think, and plan ahead.
4. If you break something, fix it.
5. If you don't know something, learn.
6. If you fall down, get back up.
7. Look in the direction you want to go, not where you don't want to go.
8. Practice mindfulness. Focus on what you're doing and do things in the correct order.
9. Practice good habits often and commit to the process.
10. Enjoy the ride.

These seem so ridiculously simple and obvious.

But, if they are that simple, why am I not practicing them all the time? Not just on the motorcycle, but off it as well?

I find I need to consciously put these practices in place. That's why we call Zen a "practice."

I'm learning how to practice Zen more, every day. Yet most people who know me would not consider me a "Zen" person, by the slang definition of the word. People use the word Zen all the time as slang for "calm" and "blissful."

People will say, "Oh, what a Zen weekend I had at the spa in Cancun." Or "My dog is so relaxed, he's got a Zen look on his face."

While that is one element of it, Zen isn't about being high on bliss without any substance. It isn't just about being a calm person. Bliss and calm are outcomes of practicing the discipline of Zen. But they aren't Zen by themselves.

Bliss is temporary and fleeting. Zen is a constant practice.

So, what does Zen really mean? And what does Zen have to do with changing habits and learning how to ride a motorcycle? And how does this relate to healing from depression and anxiety?

Riding a motorcycle did not cure me of anxiety or depression. Riding a motorcycle is not a cure for anything.

If you are suffering from anxiety or depression, riding a motorcycle won't take the place of a doctor or therapist. Riding a motorcycle is not Zen. Yet I only began to understand the concept of Zen when I started learning to ride a motorcycle.

On my fiftieth birthday, I decided to learn to ride. I was inspired by my cousin's speech at my uncle's funeral. He taught her to ride motorcycles when she was around six years old. And the principles he taught her on the motorcycles, were principles she applied to her life. She is now a successful emergency medical doctor.

My friend Jen Sincero, *New York Times* bestselling author of *You Are a Badass*, would often say, "How a person does any one thing, is how a person does everything." I was surprised to learn that this concept originated in Zen Buddhism.

The idea is this.

Say there is a person who is in the habit of procrastinating in the morning. We'll call him Bob. Bob gets distracted while he is attempting to get dressed in the morning. Bob's phone keeps dinging and he cannot ignore it. Bob's getting anxious because he's running late for his job interview. He is now distracted by his anxiety, from showing up late for the interview. Despite this, Bob gets the job. But Bob is also in the habit of hitting the snooze button in the morning, and shows up late for work. Bob also gets distracted at work, and is late with deadlines. When trying to meet a deadline, Bob ends up being late for meetings, too. Bob doesn't get fired, because he is good at what he does. However, Bob only gets a fraction of a raise during his performance review, due to him being tardy with punching in on time and work deadlines.

Let's say there is another person, named Sally, who is in the habit of meditating in the morning. Sally is in the habit of being mindful, and she doesn't get distracted when she is getting ready in the morning. Sally is in the habit of turning off the alerts on her phone. She shows up early for work, early for meetings, and meets her deadlines on time. During Sally's annual performance review, she gets the maximum increase in her salary.

How each person does one thing, is how they do everything.

And it begins on the smallest level.

Sally is in the habit of shutting off her cell phone alerts. Bob is not in the habit of shutting off his cell phone alerts.

And that one little habit makes all the difference in their lives (and their salaries).

The word Zen is a paradox. It's not something that is easy to describe. It is only understood when we figure out how to practice it. It takes an intense amount of discipline and focus to practice Zen.

And yet it is also the easiest thing in the world to do.

Zen is not found in a church, in a yoga studio, or in a mantra. We find Zen when we practice mindfulness in our approach to all the things we do.

What I learned about Zen from riding a motorcycle, is that the only thing I can do when I'm riding, is to ride. I'm not thinking about the past or the future. I'm not worrying about crashing, because I'm too busy focusing on exactly what I'm doing, as well as what the other drivers on the road are doing. I'm not praying to God on the motorcycle. Instead, being in the present and focused in the moment IS the "prayer."

Practicing Zen, to quote Alan Watts (a famous British writer and interpreter of Zen), "is to simply peel the potatoes when you are peeling potatoes." Because if you half-ass and wing one thing, you're going to half-ass and wing everything in life.

When I'm riding my motorcycle, I'm riding my motorcycle.

Practicing mindfulness, and responding instead of reacting, leads to peace of mind. Responding is practicing mindfulness. Reacting is not.

Are you focused on what you want in life? Or are you focused on what you are afraid of?

Are you reacting with fear instead of responding with wisdom?

Are you respecting where you are on your journey in life?

To quote Alan Watts again, "The only Zen you will find on a mountaintop, is the Zen you bring up there with you."

When you practice the Ten Zen Principles of Good Motorcycle Riding Habits in your daily life, you are developing good habits. Habits that give you clarity, ease your anxiety, and ground you in the present moment.

When you are living in the present, you are at peace. Even if the present situation is not a peaceful place. Good or bad, accepting where you are on your journey is one way to practice Zen.

I decided to share my personal stories of struggling with anxiety and depression because I want you to know, if you are suffering in the same way, you can find peace. I have seen every side of mental illness as the daughter of a schizophrenic, a mental health patient myself, and now as a registered nurse in psychiatric and mental health. It is possible to rise above your challenges and come out on the other side. It is possible to create the kind of life you have always wanted to live.

I wanted to share my Ten Zen Habits with you as a framework to start your own healing journey. If you are suffering, I want you to find freedom from anxiety and depression. I want you to fully experience the journey that is life, regardless of where you are on that journey.

By practicing these Ten Zen Habits, I hope that you can find a sense of healing, the way I did.

1

ZEN MOTORCYCLE HABIT #1
RESPOND TO SITUATIONS INSTEAD OF REACTING

"When you react, you are giving away your power. When you respond, you are staying in control."

—BOB PROCTOR, CANADIAN AUTHOR

How Childhood Trauma Made Me a Reactionary Person

I hate to admit this. For most of my life, I've been a reactionary person. I was pure emotion, and I often let those emotions control my life.

It started when I stopped my mother from committing suicide when I was ten years old.

When she wasn't in the grips of her demons, my mom was a petite ray of sunshine. Just under 5'2", she was like a little pixie, bubbly and creative. She was a ballet dancer and an artist. I'd look at old black-and-white ballet photos of her. In my favorite one, she's about eighteen years old. Her wavy brown hair in an up-do surrounded by a tiara. She is dressed in her ballet costume. A shiny light-colored satin bodice under a short tutu. She is wearing satin ballet slippers, laced up her calves in a crisscross pattern, standing on her tippy toes. She is staring off to the side, a longing look in her eyes. Her head is slightly turned to the right as she holds her arms out in a graceful pose. She looks like a classic Hollywood starlet.

Her demons would always seem to come back around Easter. She had suffered two late-term miscarriages. One when I was three, another when I was five. Both happened around Easter. And every Easter thereafter, she would start acting weird. She'd stare off into the distance, not hearing me. Or she'd stay in bed until the late afternoon.

Then, every Easter after I was six years old, my mother would end up in the hospital psychiatric unit. Because she had a "chemical imbalance in her brain that causes depression," according to my dad and close relatives.

Once, my mom was in the hospital on Easter Sunday when I was around seven years old. My father had forgotten it was a holiday. I woke up to see if the Easter Bunny had left me a basket of candy in the usual spot behind the living room curtains.

It wasn't there.

I immediately thought that I must have been a bad girl and the Easter Bunny skipped my house that year. I ran into my father's room and woke him up.

"The Easter Bunny didn't come. He doesn't like me anymore."

My dad tried to cover. He said, "Oh no, honey. The Easter Bunny didn't forget you. He is so busy nowadays he must've given money to Mommy in advance to buy candy with. Come on, let's look and see if we can find it."

We did find the Easter candy on the top shelf of my parent's closet. It was all still in the packaging and grocery store bags, and not at all pretty or set up in a colorful basket. The magic was gone.

"See? I told you that the Easter Bunny didn't forget you," my dad said.

The gig was up, though. I thought to myself, "Oh my god.

There is no such thing as the Easter Bunny, and I bet Santa Claus and the Tooth Fairy are bullshit, too." I began to feel like there was no real magic in the world without my best friend, my mom.

My mother was in a psychiatric unit, believing that her failed pregnancies were either demon-babies that God had saved her from, or maybe they had been like a sacrifice to God. Particularly because her first miscarriage happened on Good Friday.

It didn't help that in the early 1970s, when my mother was pregnant, movies like *Rosemary's Baby* and *It's Alive* were super popular. *Rosemary's Baby* stars a young Mia Farrow, who has the same kind of waifish look as my mother. In it, Mia plays a pregnant woman who believes her baby might not be human. *It's Alive* is a cult-classic horror film about a regular couple who give birth to a mutant baby that kills people whenever it is frightened. And apparently the mutant baby is frightened a lot. Especially by the milk man. As campy as these B-movies were, they terrified my mother.

The pro-life versus right-to-choose movements had just been born. My mother was caught in the middle. She is an American Caucasian Protestant. Not dogmatically religious. She voted for Jimmy Carter. She's not a hippie by any means. Still, she supports the women's liberation movement.

On the other hand, my father is a Filipino Catholic. He wants to be open minded, but he comes from a strict upbringing. Rebelling against his parents, he accused them of being racist when they expressed concern about him choosing a free-spirited white Protestant American woman to be his wife. Still, my mother converted to Catholicism after my parents got engaged to appease them.

Believing she was obligated to act like a good Filipino wife, she learned how to cook Filipino dishes, like Pancit with shrimp and glass noodles, or Sinigang in a lemongrass broth with pork, string beans, and potatoes. She hung an oversized three-foot-tall wooden fork and spoon on the kitchen wall for good luck. She took Catholicism seriously, but never feels a real part of the church. Overwhelmed by guilt, my father told her it was fine with him if she attended a Protestant church instead. My mother felt like she was letting down the Filipino side of the family because she just could not relate to Catholicism. In reality, none of our relatives in the United States cared what church my mother joined. Regardless, my mother was on a quest to find the perfect family church. She dragged the family to every church within a ten-mile radius of our suburban New Jersey home. Episcopalian, Methodist, Baptist, Lutheran, Greek Orthodox, Born Again; we tried them all. My father's attitude remained the same. "I like my Catholic Church. You can go to whatever church you like. It's fine. Don't worry about everything so much."

Unable to rid herself of the Catholic guilt, she started having visions of Jesus dying on the Crucifix everywhere she looked. While she was nailing a "Yard Sale" sign to a telephone pole, she realized in horror that her nails were piercing Christ, our Lord's bloody feet.

In the late 1960s, when my mother converted to Catholicism, it was taught that abortion is a mortal sin. Even if the mother's life is in danger. Even if the baby isn't going to survive the birth. Even if the baby has already died in the womb.

Even if the baby is a demon.

In her dreams, she looked at the strange baby in her arms and notices in terror it's piercing ice-blue eyes. She knew the baby was taken by the darkness, perhaps like a White Walker from "Game of Thrones."

Good Friday, 1974

When I was about three or four years old, I was not aware that my mom was over six months pregnant.

One day she began to bleed heavily.

In the hospital, the doctors couldn't detect a fetal heartbeat. My mother was becoming septic. They were at a Catholic Hospital, and there was nobody to perform the dilation and curettage surgery. So she was taken to a different hospital where her pregnancy was officially terminated.

She wondered, "Why me?" She felt vulnerable. She felt that something was fundamentally wrong with her. She felt that evil was lurking everywhere and it manifested like poisonous flowers in her womb.

Even though she did not elect to terminate the life inside her, she was still convinced she'd committed a mortal sin. In a crushing blow, the Catholic priest she sought out for comfort, told her she shouldn't have let the doctors take the baby. Even if it meant she would lose her own life.

Spring, 1980

So, it was a school night, around Easter time. I was around ten years old. I was playing at my friend Kathy's house, who wanted me to sleep over. But there was no way my parents were going to let me sleep over a friend's house on a school night.

I was so sure of it, I didn't even want to ask. Because I could hear my dad's stern voice, with his thick Filipino accent, "Les. You know better than to ask if you can sleep oh-ber on a school night. You're grounded por asking."

But Kathy was persistent.

"The worst they could do is say no. Come on, ask them. Please?" Kathy begged.

She had a point.

My mother answered after the second ring, but she sounded weird. Not like her regular bubbly, upbeat self.

"Mommy, Kathy wants to know if I can sleep over

tonight. I know it's a school night. Don't get mad. I'm just asking, okay?"

"Yes, okay…yes, that would be a good idea. You can sleep over," she responded in a voice so slow and drawn out, that it almost didn't sound like her.

That wasn't what I was expecting.

Confused, I asked, "Are you sure it's okay?" Not because I didn't want to sleep over at Kathy's, but because it was weird that she was saying yes on a school night.

And even weirder that she had said it would be a good idea.

Since when is sleeping over at a friend's house on a school night a good idea?

"Yes, you can sleep over Kathy's house, okay?" Then she mumbled something about having to go far away, so it would be good if I stayed at Kathy's.

"Bye, honey. I love you."

"What did she say?" Kathy asked, with her hands folded into a prayer, after I hung up.

"Um, she said I could sleep over."

"Yay!" Kathy clapped her hands and jumped up and down.

But I was uneasy.

"Something's not right, Kathy. I need to call my mom back."

"Nooooo." Kathy slumped down onto the couch. "What do you mean, something's not right?"

My parents had been arguing from time to time recently when they thought I was asleep. Once or twice, I'd heard my mother threaten my father. She said that she was going to leave him and move back in with her mother in Arkansas. It never happened.

While on the phone with her, when I thought I'd heard my mother say something under her breath about "going far away," I worried that she was going to her mother's house in Arkansas without me. So I called her right back.

"Mom, why did you say it would be good for me to stay over at Kathy's on a school night?"

"Because I have to go away, and it would be better if you're there."

"Why?" I asked, "Where are you going? Can I come with you?"

"No, honey, you can't come with me. I'm going far, far away."

I started to get upset.

"But why not? I want to come with you. Please don't leave me!" I begged and sobbed.

"You can't come with me," she explained, "because you'd have to…" She paused before finishing.

"You'd have to die."

I started screaming and burst into full-blown tears.

"Please don't kill yourself, Mommy! Please come pick me up right now!"

"Okay," she said reluctantly.

I got off the phone, still crying. I fell onto Kathy's living room couch. I heard my little ten-year-old voice crying and sobbing, "Oh my god, my mom was going to kill herself."

I felt awful. A dark feeling of dread came over me. It was the most out of place emotion for a ten-year-old. Like, in a split second, I was no longer a child. For some reason, I remember feeling like a thirty-year-old actress in a soap opera. It was too much drama for my mind to handle. It didn't feel real. I was feeling as if my childhood was slipping away.

Even my friend Kathy, who couldn't have been older than eleven or twelve, looked traumatized. She ran out of the living room and came back with a glass of water and a box of tissues, not knowing what else to do. I drank the water, wondering if it would somehow make me feel better. Then

Kathy's mother came into the room to find out what all the fuss was about.

I repeated to her mother what I had told Kathy. Through tears and sobs I said, "My mommy said she was going to kill herself! So, I told her not to, and so she's coming to pick me up right now!"

Kathy's mother looked stunned as well and didn't know what to say. The two of them just sat on the couch with me silent. Kathy's arm stayed around my shoulders, while I cried until my mother arrived ten minutes later.

As soon as I saw my mom, I stopped crying. I was mad. How could my mom even think of leaving me? She would rather die than be my mother?

I scolded her as if I was the parent and she was the child the entire ten-minute ride home. When we got home, I told her to call her friend Frances and ask her to come over. I needed to go to bed but was afraid to fall asleep because I worried my mom might try to kill herself again.

My father had been down the street at a neighbor's house working on their motorcycles while this was going on. He missed the whole thing. But when he came home and found out what had happened, he gave my mother an ultimatum. If she ever tried to commit suicide again, he would leave her.

After that night, whenever I'd get off the school bus, I'd run home, instead of walking. I was terrified I'd come home one day and find my mother's lifeless body.

I'd skip over the cracks in the sidewalk. Because I couldn't afford to "step on a crack and break my mother's back" when she was already suicidal.

After stopping my mother from taking her own life that night, my life became one big reaction. I could no longer just "be." There was no more responding to life. It became difficult to process new things. There was no conscious living. Just emotional reactions. Being in a state of panic became my baseline normal.

I could no longer afford to relax and just take things in life at face value anymore. The world became a scary and uncertain place. A place where if I didn't read between the lines and do something about it immediately, someone could die.

It was all "life or death" and "fight or flight." I became paranoid I'd miss something and began reading too much into things.

With my mom, I had reacted to something I didn't understand. And that reaction saved my mother's life.

This reinforced in me a false belief that I was responsible for her actions. Had I not called her back, she could have died. It would have been all my fault. So I felt like I always had to be on guard. Hypervigilant. I had to be ready to act the next time a crisis struck.

My "feelings" and impulses made decisions for me. They had helped me save my mother's life. Or so I thought.

June 2021, Los Angeles, California

"Do you have the patience to wait until your mud settles and the water is clear?"

—LAO TZU, CHINESE PHILOSOPHER

So, what is the difference between reacting and responding?

Reacting is impulsive, instinctual, and spontaneous. Reacting is not a cultivated skill. Reacting is not well thought out.

The other night, I threw the television remote control at my husband. He was chastising me about how I was flipping through channels. This was a reaction. A response would have been to hand the remote control to him and ask him what he wanted to watch.

Grabbing the front brake on a motorcycle and skidding out is a reaction. Staying on the throttle and swerving out of the way of danger is a response.

Reactions can lead to hurt feelings in life, and a hurt body on a motorcycle.

Reacting was important for our survival back in the days when we were living in trees and caves. Our instinctive reactions kept us from getting eaten alive by lions or other beasts. The fight or flight response kept us alive when we were at the bottom of the food chain. But reacting, particularly in the modern world, can be reckless, according to Hans Selye (1907 – 1982), endocrinologist and founder of the Stress Theory.

In the modern world, these reactions are not always appropriate.

When we experience anxiety in a stressful situation, we are rarely in immediate danger. Like, if your boss reprimands you at work. You're not actually in danger of dying. Just take the criticism constructively and do better next time.

But our bodies may react as if we are in immediate danger.

Responding is derived from the word responsible. Responding is a well thought out, conscious, mindful action. It means we take the time to cultivate skills and learn a process. It means we take the time to consciously process information before acting on it.

Off the motorcycle, it means we aren't jumping to conclusions during a conversation.

Being reactive and impulsive does not lead to spontaneous freedom. Being reactive on a motorcycle will often lead to accidents and injury.

Even into my adulthood, my triggers for fear were strong. I'd run away from situations instead of learning the skills to manage them. I'd end relationships that I didn't want to end just because I was scared. I'd quit jobs as soon as I felt insecure or made a mistake. I'd sabotage opportunities because I didn't think I could handle them.

This is how I lived a reactionary life.

I realized early on, my instincts on a motorcycle are all wrong. I needed to develop skills, not reactions. My instincts had me grabbing the front brake on the motorcycle whenever I was afraid of anything. And every time I reacted this way, my motorcycle and I ended up on the ground. Motorcyclists are constantly building muscle memory to override their reactions.

When we learn to respond to situations in life, instead of reacting to them, we begin to create conscious habits that serve us.

Instead of making fearful reactions that might hurt us, we allow our wisdom and intellect to guide us. We consciously want to create healthy habits that will become healthy responses.

This is one way to practice Zen.

2

ZEN MOTORCYCLE HABIT #2
UNDERSTAND AND RESPECT YOUR OWN LIMITATIONS, AND SET YOUR OWN PACE

"Anxiety, the next gumption trap, is sort of the opposite of ego. You're so sure you'll do everything wrong you're afraid to do anything at all. Often this, rather than 'laziness,' is the real reason you find it hard to get started."

—ROBERT PIRSIG, ZEN AND THE ART OF
MOTORCYCLE MAINTENANCE

Why I gave up on motorcycle riding the first time I tried to learn

My cousin Vivian stood in front of her father's casket. My Filipino Uncle Pete, who lived well into his eighties, has died.

"I've been riding motorcycles pretty much my whole life. And my dad is the one who taught me how," Vivian said.

I was surprised to hear that she was still riding motorcycles forty years later.

Motorcycle riding was something our Filipino fathers loved to do. Like Vivian, my introduction to motorcycles was through my Filipino father. Around the same time Vivian was learning to ride, I took my first ride ever with my dad on the back of his champagne-colored 1980 BMW R65 at nine years old. It was a classic-styled naked-bike with a brown leather seat. Wearing my candy-apple blue helmet with my arms wrapped around my dad's waist, we rode down Old Hook Road, in New Jersey. Past the reservoir, deer grazed in the meadows. My dad would check in on me at every stop. He turned his head and in a voice muffled by his full-face helmet, he'd ask, "You okay?" I'd nod my head, yes. My face hurt from smiling so hard.

"Okay, then, hold on tight and don't let go."

Vivian's father, my Uncle Pete, was the first of our Filipino fathers to immigrate to the United States in the 1960s. He grew up with my dad in Manila. They are first cousins, but lived in the same home, like brothers. My Uncle Pete's father was poor and lived in the provinces. The good schools were in the city of Manila, so if you ever wanted to go to college, you had to attend school there. So my uncles Pete and Cesar lived with my dad and grandfather most of their childhood.

I told my dad that it was Vivian and Uncle Pete's fault that I bought a motorcycle at age fifty. My dad said, "No, Les. I was the first one to get a motorcycle. He got into motorcycles because of me."

It's true, my dad was the first one in the family to get into motorcycles. My grandfather bought him a Vespa for his fifteenth birthday.

My Uncle Pete became a doctor. He wanted to expand his horizons and leave the Philippines. He and my dad dreamed of moving to America and riding motorcycles together. Pete was the first to embark on this dream. He finally moved to Long Island, New York after becoming an Ob-Gyn. He married a German lady, my Aunt Hannelore, who also became a doctor. They eventually settled down in an affluent white suburb of New Jersey. Soon after, my cousins Michael, Margarita, and Vivian were born.

My Uncle Pete convinced my father to join him in New York in 1966. While in graduate school for engineering, my dad lived with my Uncle Pete's family, and after graduating and a few entry-level jobs later, he started working his dream position as a quality control engineer for Mercedes-Benz.

When my parents met, my mother was pursuing a career as a ballet dancer in New York City. My Dad was living in a bachelor pad apartment in Queens with some other guys at the time. Apparently, it was a real dive. They even used the pages from *Playboy* magazines to cover their dismal, ugly walls. Not long after my parents met at a party, my mother's ballet company declared bankruptcy. Her dancing career was in peril and she was afraid. Back then, there weren't a lot of options for women.

She married my father in September of 1969 in New York City. Nine months later, I was born.

My Uncle Pete had a younger brother, Cesar, who followed in my Uncle Pete and my dad's footsteps to America. He and his wife, my Aunt Tita, had two daughters, my cousins Mary Ellen and Maria Victoria. Mary Ellen was six months older than me and Maria Victoria was six months younger. Margarita was the oldest, Vivian was the youngest, and I was right smack in the middle of the five of us. We grew up like siblings, like our fathers did.

August 2019, West Covina, California

At my Uncle Pete's funeral, Vivian told her story.

"Back in the 1970s, before bicycle helmet and seatbelt laws existed, I think I was about eight years old [note: she was actually five] when my older brother Michael and I decided to take my dad's mini-bikes out on the street. Without asking, of course.

"While we were tooling around on this side street, we saw a police car with its lights on in the distance. And we totally freaked out. I'm sure the cop didn't even see us. But we thought, 'Oh no! We are going to get arrested.'

"So, Michael says 'quick Vi! Into the woods.'

"I tried to ride the motorcycle into the woods. But I ended up hitting the curb and flying over the handlebars. I messed up the bike pretty bad, as well as my face. There was blood and motorcycle parts on the ground.

"Michael said, 'Oh, man. Dad is gonna kill us." Then says, 'Okay, let me talk to him. I'll take the blame for everything.'

"So we go home and Michael starts telling my dad how we were riding the dirt-bikes in the street. And how we were trying to escape the cops by riding into the woods."

"My dad is trying to look serious. But I notice he's trying to prevent the corner of his mouth from smiling. He is really trying not to laugh. I realize he is actually proud of us. Thinking of us two kids trying to outrun the cops on motorcycles.

"But he says in a stern voice, 'Okay, go clean yourselves up. We'll talk about this tomorrow.'

"So, the next day, my dad comes into my room and says, 'Vivian, I need to talk to you in the garage.' And I'm thinking, 'Oh man, this is it, I am so dead. I'm going to get grounded for life.' But instead, my dad says, 'Vivian, you messed up the motorcycle. So we have to fix it now. If you want to ride motorcycles, you need to learn how to fix them. You need to learn the right way.'

'We're going to the store to get some parts. Then you're going to help me fix it.

'And then you have to get back on it, or else you might be afraid to ever ride motorcycles again.'"

Vivian is now a well-accomplished emergency medical physician. She is the Regional Medical Director of a large, well-known hospital system in the San Francisco Bay area. The lessons my Uncle Pete taught Vivian, were lessons she ended up carrying with her for her entire life. They were the skills that helped her become a successful physician. That story made me sad that I had given up so soon the first time I tried to learn to ride a motorcycle.

New Jersey, June 1994

In my early twenties, my first serious boyfriend, Ted, and his roommate, Greg, thought it would be a great idea to teach me how to ride a motorcycle. Greg owned this little yellow 50cc Yamaha YSR motorcycle that was the perfect size for me. I thought it would be so cool. Motorcycle riding was something I thought I should learn to do. My cousins, my uncle, and even my Dad were riders.

The two of them took me to a parking lot where I started learning to shift gears. This bike was super light. I could pick it up myself. And both my feet touched the ground when I sat on the seat. But, in New Jersey, there are only a handful of months when the weather is good for riding. Ted wanted to ride around on his 1993 GSX-R, and Greg wanted to go riding when the weather was nice, too. Ted had just bought his new motorcycle the summer before. The first time he took it out, he had skidded out on some gravel and ended up in a patch of grass. His brand-new bike nearly totaled.

Ted was bruised, but not broken. Luckily he understood the importance of wearing full motorcycle gear. He came out of the accident without any scratches, just bruises. But, by the time they fixed his bike, the summer of 1993 was over and he had barely gotten two rides in.

So the following summer, when I needed to be practicing, Ted wanted to ride his GSX-R, and I ended up spending a lot more time on the back of Ted's GSX-R than learning to ride. It was a great feeling, being on the back, with my arms around him. We'd take late-night rides after midnight when I'd get off from my waitressing job. Flying through the night under the stars, the full moon would shine on us as we weaved through Harriman State Park, deer grazing in the grass lifting their heads up to watch us as we rode by.

So I didn't get enough practice time in, and although I had passed the written exam with flying colors, I panicked during the DMV road test and failed. Going too slow, looking down, putting my foot down while weaving through cones, and when I tried to brake, I either broke too soon or too late. It was too scary. I figured that motorcycle riding was something I "just wasn't good at."

In reality, I just hadn't practiced enough. Rather than keep learning and trying, I let myself become discouraged, and resigned myself to riding on the back. I felt like I was not talented enough and too nervous to cultivate riding skills, and just gave up.

I had always seen my cousins Vivian and Margarita as so fearless. But it was my Uncle Pete who had taught them to be that way. I just figured people were either brave or they weren't. I didn't realize that bravery was something that could be learned.

My Uncle Pete wanted my cousins Vivian and Margarita to grow up to be James Bond Girls. He also wanted them to be beauty queens. But he made them change the oil in their own cars. He taught them to ride motorcycles, to drive sports cars with manual transmissions, and how to shoot BB guns. He encouraged their independence. Then, in the same breath, he would warn them against becoming "old maids."

When I saw Margarita in San Diego last summer, she was thrilled to learn that I was planning on getting a motorcycle and finally learning to ride. She told me a story about how Uncle Pete taught her how to drive a car with a manual transmission.

"He showed up at my school in a Porsche when I had just

gotten my permit," Margarita told me. "And he was like, 'Okay, Ma'Grita, let's drive the Porsche.'

"So there I am, a junior high school kid in this Porsche. I'm trying to get it into first gear and I'm just stalling out. All the kids are mocking me. They're beeping their horns at me. The whole parking lot is backed up, and everyone's like sarcastically screaming at me, 'Oh, Margarita, you're so cool in that Porsche!'

"I look over at my dad. He's got a smirk on his face. He's just like, 'Well, you better figure out how to get it into first gear, or they are just going to keep making fun of you.' And that's pretty much how I learned to drive a stick shift."

I find something so funny about these two memories. I doubt my cousins realized the significance of them at the time they occurred. Not in the sense of a birthday. Or a wedding, or christening, or graduation, or some life event usually marked by an occasion. Vivian crashed the motorcycle. My uncle taught her to get up after she'd had fallen. He taught her to fix what she broke, and to learn what she didn't know. Then he taught Margarita not to give up under pressure when she stalled the Porsche in the school parking lot.

New Jersey, 1970s

At the grocery store one day with my mom, not long after she had been discharged from the hospital after having her first round of electric shock therapy, we ran into one of my mother's friends in the produce aisle. I recognized the woman right away. A petite, dark-skinned woman from India, she was the mother of one of my classmates.

"Oh, hi Lynn!" The woman smiled, happy to run into my mother. "I've been trying to get in touch with you for the past month or so. How have you been?"

"I'm sorry. I don't remember you."

The smile immediately faded from the woman's face.

"What do you mean?" the woman asked.

Even I was surprised to hear my mother say this.

"I was in the hospital," my mother explained. "They did a procedure on me. It made me lose a lot of my memories. I'm so sorry."

Both my mother and the woman looked like they were about to break into tears.

"I'm so sorry to hear that. My name is Samita. You met me at our children's school back in September."

"I'm sorry, I don't remember that." My mom barely was able to get enough of a breath to get those words out.

After the woman walked away, my mother stared at the various heads of lettuce and stalks of celery for a few moments. Her face became distorted with grief as she turned away from the produce, took my hand, and left her shopping cart in the aisle. When we got into her car, she cried and said, "I didn't want electro-shock therapy, but the doctors convinced your father it would help. It was supposed to make me forget all the bad things. Instead, I still remember all the bad things, and I can't remember any of the good things!" She pounded her fists into the steering wheel and cried while I sat next to her in the passenger seat, numb.

After one too many incidents of my mother having meltdowns in grocery store parking lots, or fainting in the middle of the fabric store when a new medication she'd been put on didn't agree with her, my parents started leaving me at my Uncle Pete's house over the summer.

When I was growing up, we spent just about every weekend at my Uncle Pete's house. It was a large ranch-sized house, with a huge front yard, and a backyard that extended into the woods. A collection of ten cars, including a dysfunctional 1960s rusted Porsche and a 1972 Mercedes-Benz with no transmission, and countless bicycles, dirt-bikes, mini-bikes, scooters, motorcycles, and mopeds spilled out of the extra-large quadruple-sized garage into the long driveway. All my cousins and the kids from the neighborhood played Marco Polo in the in-ground pool, and everyone cheated. But, surprise, I was the only one who ever got caught.

Every summer, I ended up as a bonus sister in my uncle's house. And I really was like a sister. Of course, this included bickering and all. When Margarita was becoming a teenager, Vivian and I were about seven and nine years old. Sometimes Vivian and I would unintentionally drive her crazy.

Snooping around Margarita's room was one of my favorite things to do. I'd convince Vivian to play in her room with me. Usually, I'd end up breaking something, because I'm a klutz. Like the time I ripped apart her Chinese finger cuffs because I couldn't figure out how to get out of them. Poor Margarita would get so agitated. The thing that really drove Margarita crazy was this song Vivian and I invented. We'd sing it really loud when we were looking for each other. Bellowing from one end of the house to the other, we'd sing.

I'd begin: "Viviannnn! I neeed youuuuu! Like a flowerrrr! Needs the suuuun!"

And she'd sing back: "I'm hereeee! My flooooweerrr! Where are youuuuu!??"

Margarita would groan: "Ugggh. Shut up! That's so annoying."

My Uncle bought a grand piano when we were kids. Vivian knew how to play one song on it: "The Entertainer" by Scott Joplin, from the movie *The Sting*. She'd play it over and over and over and over. Until Margarita would scream, "Achhhh! I can't take it anymore! I'm so sick of that song. Stop playing it."

Poor Margarita. We weren't trying to drive her crazy. But Vivian and I would sometimes get on her nerves.

When my mother was having really bad acute psychotic episodes, staying with my cousins took me away from the drama and the chaos at home. I could have a normal child-hood at my Uncle Pete's. My cousins and I would spend hours and hours in the swimming pool. Then Uncle Pete would let us watch James Bond movies as we sat on the carpet of the living room in our damp bathing suits. My cousins and I would play pool all night in the basement and then fall asleep next to the pool table in the cool basement at night to avoid the hot, humid New Jersey summer nights.

Then, in the early 1980s, my Uncle Pete had a mid-life crisis. He moved his family from that house in the wealthy suburban New Jersey neighborhood to West Covina, California. The extent of this loss turned out to be massive. I didn't realize what a loss this was going to be, when I lost my cousins. They were like siblings to me. My Uncle Pete's home in New Jersey was a safe haven, and my cousins were my functional siblings. I lost that too.

One summer day, I remember my family pulling up to Uncle Pete's house. There was a Winnebago in the driveway and he had a big dog with him, maybe a Collie or Labrador, that I'd never seen before. He explained how he'd fallen in love with California and was going there no matter what. If my Aunt Hannelore didn't want to come, he would leave her. So my Aunt resigned from the hospital where she worked, giving up her tenure to follow her husband West.

Margarita thrived in California. Voted prom queen, she graduated from high school and attended UCLA. On the other hand, Vivian had a harder time. She was alone in their house in West Covina when the Whittier Earthquake struck. Less than ten miles from the epicenter, Vivian was terrified and alone. Eventually, she would go on to become a physician specializing in disaster medicine. My cousin Michael was already off at college in Florida.

Unfortunately, my Uncle Pete and my Aunt Hannelore's marriage did not survive the move. So, when they separated, my Uncle Pete moved out of the family house.

One night, my cousins Vivian and Margarita were alone at home in West Covina. They heard something outside. At first they thought it was coyotes. Then they thought they heard someone walking around the perimeter of the house in the dark. Margarita heard rustling in the bushes. She saw the figure of a man.

"Vi. There's some strange man lurking around outside. Go get my BB gun."

Vivian gets the BB gun and hands it to Margarita. Margarita has her target in sight and points the gun out of the window. She is about to pull the trigger when they hear a man's voice with a thick Filipino accent cry out, "Ma'Grita! Don't choot me! It's your dad!"

"Oh my god, Dad? What the heck are you doing out there in the dark?"

"You know, Dad was really proud of you that time you almost shot him, Rita." Vivian commented some thirty years later at a family barbeque in San Diego.

Yeah, I bet he was thinking, "I did it. I raised two Bond Girls."

So Uncle Pete continued to raise my cousins to be Bond Girls. But, I was not raised to be a Bond Girl by my father. He was too busy struggling with my mother's mental illness. I was starting to get really fearful about things.

I have a memory of my cousin Vivian jumping onto a raft in the swimming pool. She was standing on it, rocking back and forth on it as if she was surfing. For some reason, it scared the living crap out of me. I was so afraid she was going to fall down and drown. I have no idea why, because if she fell, she would just fall into the water. Of course she knew how to swim. We all did. But I had the look of fear in my eyes. So fearful, in fact, Vivian remembers it to this day. I recently brought up this memory to Vivian. She said, "I totally remember exactly what you are talking about. You looked terrified and I didn't know why."

The constant instability at home with my mother going in and out of the hospital was taking its toll on me. Her mental illness was confusing, and I never knew which fears of mine were based in reality.

This was the start of my clinical anxiety.

Los Angeles, California, September 2020

After hearing Vivian's speech at my uncle's funeral in 2019, I became inspired. I wanted to try to learn to ride a motorcycle again. The following summer, I signed up for a Motorcycle Safety Foundation (MSF) course, and earned my motorcycle license. Still, I was the first person to drop a motorcycle in the class. I dropped the Yamaha V-Star. Then they put me on a 2012 Zero XU electric motorcycle, and I dropped that one, too.

Three drops and you are out. Then you have to reschedule and pay an extra $100 to retake the class.

One of the instructors gave me the option of taking the class on the Zero XU, an electric motorcycle with the automatic transmission. She thought I might feel less distracted, and she said I could learn to shift gears at another time. I felt like it was a cop-out, but at the same time, I didn't want to be the one to hold up the class. I wasn't getting the hang of the clutch as quickly as the other students were. Something that might have made me give up in the past. But now I didn't want the fact that I needed more time to learn to prevent me from finishing the course.

Well, I finished the course. It turns out, I ended up passing the class with flying colors.

"Can I tell you a secret? You were my best student," the MSF Instructor said to me under his breath when he was handing me my certificate. How could I be the best student when I hadn't mastered shifting gears? And had also dropped two motorcycles?

According to my teacher, I was his best student because I was respecting my boundaries. Honoring my limitations, going at my own pace, my ego stayed tucked away. Not everyone in the class had passed. I felt great about myself. And so proud when I got my motorcycle license. It is completely outside of my comfort zone.

As I continued my motorcycle-riding education, I began to keep a video diary of myself on YouTube. Meant as a way to prevent myself from getting discouraged, the videos served as a reminder of my progress. Never in my wildest dreams, did I expect anyone to watch the videos. At the start, my subscribers totaled a grand number of three. One was a coworker of mine who also was learning to ride. I never expected anyone else to watch those videos.

My brush with internet celebrity happened one day when I posted a thirty-six-second video of myself tooling around a parking lot on my motorcycle. Within a couple hours, it had gotten 18,000 views.

I thought for sure the spirit of my Uncle Pete had hacked the YouTube algorithm from beyond the grave. It's still a mystery as to how that boring little video got so many views.

Unfortunately, my newfound popularity resulted in me not respecting the process again. As I chit-chatted with other YouTubers who had recently learned to ride, I watched them move forward in leaps and bounds on their electric motorcycles, careening up and down the open roads like Jack Nicholson in Easy Rider, while I was suffering from a case of FOMO.

I found myself, once again, not respecting where I was in the process. One of my subscribers had pointed out to me that we had bought our motorcycles around the same time. He had already put 1500 miles on his motorcycle, and I had barely put 150 miles on mine. I was struggling to get out of my driveway. No, literally.

My driveway is super steep and skinny, with a blind spot. There's not a lot of room to maneuver, especially when you don't have those skills in the first place. That meant limiting practicing to when my husband was free. I relied on him to escape that driveway. So I was only putting about five or six measly miles on my bike per week. This is the point where I'd usually quit.

Feeling so far behind my peers always left me feeling depressed and inferior. It's so hard to simply accept where I am and work from there. It's getting past the self-doubt that has always been the biggest challenge for me. When I was shopping for my first street bike, I was having anxiety about learning how to shift gears. I worried that I'd be so focused on shifting gears, I'd have a hard time paying attention to traffic. I was concerned about learning to turn. I was concerned about learning how to keep my bike upright when stopping. I was concerned about using the brakes properly.

I wanted to learn to ride a motorcycle. Yet I was also thinking about the things I didn't want to deal with if I didn't have to: I didn't want to have to deal with shifting gears, being afraid, feeling distracted by anxiety. I decided to get an electric motorcycle like the one I successfully rode in the MSF course and I scheduled a test ride. Unfortunately they no longer made the old XU model I rode in class. But the new Zero S model turned out to be too tall for me. I couldn't even get it off the kickstand when I sat on it. The dealer said they could lower the bike as well as shave down the seat for me. So I went for it.

I bought the Zero S without test riding it.

I wasn't respecting where I was on my journey when I was shopping for my first bike. I wasn't looking in the direction that I wanted to go. I was focusing on what I didn't want instead. I wasn't respecting my boundaries and limitations. I wasn't setting my own pace.

What I didn't want was to make things more difficult for myself than necessary. I wanted to avoid the anxiety and panic I associated with learning to shift gears on a motorcycle. I was focusing on not wanting to be afraid. Not wanting to get overwhelmed. I should have been focusing on, "I want to learn to ride a motorcycle."

I replaced the challenge of learning to shift gears on the motorcycle with a different challenge. One of the downfalls of a motorcycle with an automatic transmission is that it's always in gear. So when I'd hit the throttle unintentionally when trying to brake (also sometimes known as "The Whiskey Throttle"), the bike would take off! Unprepared for the amount of torque this bike had behind it, I'd end up on the ground every time.

I replaced one scary challenge (shifting gears) with another scary challenge (the Whiskey Throttle). I wasn't able to avoid being scared or being challenged. If you want to learn to ride a motorcycle, you will experience fear and anxiety. You will need to learn to do things you've never done before. You will need to override some of your instincts and use your skills. You will need to learn to control the motorcycle, and this takes just as long as learning to shift gears.

You must respect where you are on your life's journey. Whether it's learning to ride a motorcycle, learning to crawl, learning to walk, learning a new trade, learning to get back up after a fall, learning to hike, learning to surf, or learning a new job. Trying to cut corners will only result in having to backtrack later. There is no avoiding the occasional feelings of inadequacy, fear, or anxiety associated with learning something new.

So, what did I learn? That there are no shortcuts to the process, and there are no shortcuts in life either. What do I want more? To learn to ride or to not be scared? There is no way to learn how to ride a motorcycle without experiencing some healthy fears at some point. It can't be avoided; it can only be overcome.

It may take me longer to learn certain things than most people. But who am I competing with, exactly? I wanted to learn to ride a motorcycle for no other reason than because I wanted to. I still get frustrated and feel bad when I am not picking up something as quickly as I believe I should.

It may take me a lot longer than other people, but I'm not like other people.

I've learned to respect where I am and take my time. I'm on nobody's timeclock but my own.

3

ZEN MOTORCYCLE HABIT #3

BE PREPARED: THINK AND PLAN AHEAD

*"It is better to be prepared for an opportunity and not have one,
than to have an opportunity and not be prepared."*

— WHITNEY M. YOUNG JR., CIVIL RIGHTS ACTIVIST

**How I did one thing, is how I did everything: how living
impulsively led to financial issues and other problems**

I cried on my bedroom floor the day I graduated from college.
I had no idea what I was going to do with myself. Not outside
of "Hopefully I become a rich and famous singer so I can
afford everything I want in the world."

I didn't have a plan.

New Jersey, Fall 1988

It's my freshman year in college. My friends are figuring out
what they want to be when they grow up. Meanwhile, I am
still struggling to figure out what I should major in. Currently
majoring in visual arts, I don't think I'm good enough at
anything to make a living at it. Bad at math. Bad at science.

Bad at typing. Mediocre at drawing and painting. I'm feeling like I have no skills that I could translate into a money-making career.

Sherri lived in the dorm room right next door to mine. She was majoring in business when we first met. By the end of our freshman year, Sherri decided business wasn't for her, and she was going to become a nurse. She was so certain and happy about it. She had a solid plan for her future. Meanwhile, I spent my time plucking away on a pink Ibanez electric guitar. Sherri is a well-accomplished neonatal nurse now. She travels and surfs all over the place.

We met in the first semester of our freshman year in college. Her dorm room was next to mine on the third floor, and I had one of those mini-fridges in my room. Sherri asked if she could store her Budweiser beers in my fridge. I was welcome to help myself to some, if I let her.

It was hard to relate to the other girls in my school, but maybe Sherri and I would become friends. She wasn't snobby or into designer clothes. Not one to wear Calvin Klein jeans, she wore classic Levi's with little moccasins, and a Baja hoodie (aka "drug rug") over a tie-dyed T-shirt. She was a Dead-Head and had stickers of the Dancing Bears on the back window of her car.

I would always keep a box of saltine crackers in my room. Less than a dollar a box, they were great to snack on if you were drunk or hungover. Sherri would always ask if she could have some of my saltines, and I'd always say yes. After all, she let me drink her beer.

One day I came home from class, and Sherri was in my room eating my crackers. I literally walked in as her hand was elbow-deep in a box of saltines. She looked up at me, wide-eyed and surprised.

"Oh shit, caught in the act."

I just started cracking up. Then Sherri started laughing,

too. She said, "Well, I knew you were going to say yes, anyway."

That's when I knew we were going to be friends for life.

When we came back from Winter Break, Sherri and I found out our roommates were not returning to school. We bonded right away when I decided to move into her dorm room. While unpacking our clothes, Sherri picked up a 1980s-style white belt and inspected the chunky jewels and metal spikes that covered it.

"Oh wow, I wonder what Eric would think if I wore something like this," she wondered, referring to her boyfriend back home.

"I bought that because it reminded me of Ann Wilson from the band Heart," I explained.

Sherri had a lot of hippie-style tops and T-shirts with album covers of the Grateful Dead on them. I picked up a cotton shirt covered in a red and orange Indian-style bohemian pattern and held it up to myself. "I've never worn anything like this before," I said, looking in the mirror.

"Oh, I bought that at a Dead show," Sherri explained.

We wore the same size clothing, but our styles were totally different. I was from Northern New Jersey, near all the shopping malls and the George Washington Bridge, where the girls dressed like Madonna and the boys dressed like Jon Bon Jovi. My long black hair was permed into tight ringlets, held in place with a 99-cent bottle of Aqua Net Hairspray. Sherri was from Southern New Jersey, near the beaches and Philadelphia, where the girls dressed like bohemians and the boys dressed like surfers. She wore her long blond hair down or in braids. Pretty soon, we were swapping clothes and creating various versions of bohemia fashion with an eighties rock and roll twist.

Of course, all this experimenting with each other's clothing made it difficult to get dressed and get out of the dorms in a timely fashion on Saturday nights. We'd hang out with these three guys we became friends with who lived on the other side of campus named Mike, Steve, and Rob. Mike and Rob had girlfriends who would visit our campus on the weekends, and they were super cool girls, too. Steve had a girlfriend in another State. I had a crush on Steve.

Steve was one of those guys who had no idea how good looking he was. He had light brown shaggy hair and piercing blue eyes. He wore a long vintage store–bought trench coat over his jeans. He was a hipster in 1989 before hipsters were a thing.

Already running late to meet up with the guys at The Green Parrot, a reggae bar in Neptune, New Jersey, Sherri looked at herself in the mirror and made a face. Wearing her usual Dead Head garb, she said, "I don't feel like wearing this."

I had on a pair of white jeans and a black top and was kind of feeling bored with my look as well. Sherri tossed off her drug-rug poncho and put on the cotton shirt covered in the red and orange Indian-style Bohemian pattern. She looked at herself for a minute.

"No, not this one either." She tossed it off, so I took off my boring black top and put her Bohemian top on over my white jeans and white-fringed boots. Then I added the chunky white belt.

"Oh, cool. I like this look." I was pretty much wearing all white and it reminded me of something one of the women in the group the Bangles might wear. "Mind if I wear this?"

"Oh, wow! I like that on you! You can keep that shirt."

Sherri was on her third outfit, so I sat down and drank one of her Budweiser beers. Then she tried on a fourth outfit, so I had another beer. Several beers and outfits later, Sherri was finally happy with her fifth or sixth ensemble. We made our way down to the first floor and were about to walk out of the lobby when Sherri said, "Oh shit! I left my wallet upstairs!"

While I waited at the bottom of the stairs of our dorm for

what seemed like forever, Sherri finally made her way back down to where I'd been waiting, and was wearing her drug-rug poncho over her favorite pair of Levi's again. The same outfit she had started with.

"You have got to be fucking kidding me!" I was annoyed but burst into laughter. Not realizing how buzzed I'd gotten from the Budweiser beers, I started laughing uncontrollably as we walked toward the parking lot. Just then, my white-fringed boots slid on some wet, muddy grass and after almost doing a split, I landed in a puddle of mud in my white jeans.

"You have got to be fucking kidding me!" I screamed for the second time that evening, as Sherri doubled over with laughter.

So it was back to the third floor so I could change my clothes. Sherri stopped in the mirror for a moment, but I pushed her out the door.

Every Tuesday night, Sherri and I would hang out with Mike, Steve, and Rob and drink a bottle of Absolut vodka. We would never have any money left over to buy juice or soda to mix it with, so we'd just do shots, and then share a single can of Pepsi to chase it down. We'd call it "Sherri and Leslie's Tuesday Night Absolut-fest."

During one particular Absolut-fest, I felt like Steve was hitting on me, but thought I must be mistaken because someone as cool as Steve certainly would not be interested in a little dork like me. We were all in a dorm suite, which consisted of three bedrooms and a living room with a shared bathroom. Terrible at reading social cues, I asked Sherri to come to the bathroom with me so we could analyze the Steve situation. Plus, I was feeling like I needed to throw up.

"Steve is totally hitting on you!" Sherri confirmed while we were in the bathroom.

"Omigod, he is? I thought he was, but I can't tell because I'm too drunk! I think I need to throw up," I said as I began heaving into the toilet.

Sherri and I continued our conversation while I vomited into the toilet as if everything was normal.

"Yeah, he's so hot. You should totally go for it," Sherri said.

"Really [raaalph]? You think I should, like, jump him [choke, cough, spit]?"

"Omigod, yes. I would. You should totally just jump him."

Unbeknownst to us, Mike, Steve, and Rob could hear every single word we spoke, and every time I wretched into the toilet, clear as a bell. They laughed in silent hysterics and pretended they hadn't heard a thing after we emerged from the bathroom.

"Why are you guys so quiet all of the sudden?" I asked the three of them as they sat there motionless with their hands over their mouths.

Steve stood up and ran into the hallway giggling, then popped his head back into the doorway and said, "Come here, Leslie, we need to talk." He took my hand, led me down the hall to his dorm room, and the next thing I knew, we were in our underwear on his twin-sized bed, rolling around, sweaty and drunk.

The next morning in the cafeteria, Mike and Rob were eating a New Jersey signature breakfast: Taylor ham and cheese on a roll with coffee. Although they were trying to contain themselves, as soon as they saw me, they started laughing.

"Hey guys!"

The two of them turned red and continued laughing.

"Wait. What's so funny?" I asked.

"You do know, that when you're in the dorm bathrooms, everyone in the living room can hear every fart, sneeze and cough happening in there?" Rob asked me.

Suddenly, I became flushed with embarrassment.

"So…could you hear everything that Sherri and I were talking about last night when we were in the bathroom?"

They both burst into laughter, while Rob mocked me in a fake, high-pitched voice, "Omigod! Steve is so hot [raallllph]! Should I jump him [raaaaalph]!?"

Oh. My. God. Everyone, including Steve, had heard everything. I was mortified. I spent the next week avoiding Steve at all costs. However, whenever I'd run into Mike or Rob on campus, they'd start mock-vomiting and laughing.

Needing a break from my humiliation on campus, I invited Sherri to drive to Long Beach Island with me one weekend so I could introduce her to surfing, as well as to my surfer friends, Butch, Morty, and Jimmy. I'd met them the first summer I tried to learn to surf in Long Beach Island.

Long Beach Island, New Jersey, Summer 1987

I was struggling to learn how to ride the surfboard my dad had bought me for my seventeenth birthday. It was a bummer practicing by myself, as it was a bit scary. So, since there were no boys in my all-girls Catholic school, and I was not one of the cool kids, I adopted this group of local Long Beach Island surfers as my main social circle. My winter weekends were spent down the shore with this sad motley crew of local boys whose families were so poor, half the time I'd try to call any one of them up on the phone, it would be disconnected. So I'd often spontaneously drive down there and knock on their doors to see who was home. They were always so grateful when I'd visit.

Long Beach Island is the place where the rich and wealthy families of New Jersey would spend their summers. The locals there were poor as fuck, though. The rich kids would come down there for the summer on Memorial Day and would fully embrace the local kids as their best friends. During the summer, there was no class divide among the teenagers. The rich kids would bond with, and swear lifelong friendship to, the impoverished locals. Then, the second after Labor Day was over, the rich kids would disappear as if the local kids never existed. Long Beach Island looks like a ghost town from October to May. Often, I'd joke that if you were in Long Beach Island in the winter and there had been a nuclear war, you wouldn't be able to tell.

After I introduced Sherri to my surfing group, they fell in love with her. Especially Mike Morton, or "Morty." "He's the best surfer in Long Beach Island," my friend Butch told me the first night we met one summer after my friends and I picked him up hitchhiking through Surf City.

Morty was obsessed with Sherri and kept showing up at our dorm room in the middle of the night. Unfortunately, he would bring my ex-boyfriend Jimmy with him. My ex, who I referred to as "Jimmy in the Orange Beetle" (because he told me he was living in his Orange Volkswagen Bug after getting kicked out of his house), had broken my heart the summer before.

New Jersey, The Mid-1980s

I'd fallen for Jimmy's pitiful story the first time I met him in front of the Beach Haven 7-11 when I was sixteen years old. We made eye contact when he was shoving a bunch of clothes into his trunk (which on a Volkswagen Beetle, is in the front). I remember seeing dress shoes, some tie-dyed shirts, a wetsuit, some beach towels, a white button-down shirt and a tie, a Rastafarian-looking poncho and a pair of dress shoes before he quickly shoved everything in and slammed down the hood. Then he leaned against his car with his arms crossed in front of his chest and looked right at me with his sad almond-shaped ocean-blue eyes. He looked like a young Christian Slater. I don't remember how we started talking, but he told me he wanted to be a professional surfer and that his parents were against it. So, he said, his father told him to get out. Then he threw all his belongings out of his bedroom window and told him to go ahead and try to make a living as a surfer. So now he was living in his orange Volkswagen Beetle.

Later, I found out, none of that had actually happened to Jimmy. It happened to Morty. Jimmy just thought it was a great story to use to try to pick up girls. And, well, it worked on me. I dated him for about five days, and then he gave me a sob story about how his lifestyle, the orange Beetle, possibly going to San Diego, estranged from his parents... "I just don't think I'm in the right place to have a girlfriend, living in my car and all..." Then he kissed me goodbye and drove off into the sunset. I was hooked.

In the mid-1980s, we didn't have cell phones, or email addresses, or social media to stay connected with each other. Since Jimmy was living in his Orange Beetle, there wasn't even a land line that I could dial him up on, either. After that fateful night in front of the 7-11, my sixteen-year-old mind was made up though: As soon as I got my driver's license the following spring, I was going to find Jimmy in the orange Beetle and ask him to the prom. I spent the entire winter dreaming of how it might go down when I'd run into him. I'd be seventeen by then, with my own car. I was begging my father to buy me a white Volkswagen Cabriolet convertible. Maybe my boobs would finally grow in by then, too. We'd recognize each other as we passed by one another on the dunes at East Atlantic Avenue, the street in Harvey Cedars where Jimmy parked when he surfed. Our eyes would meet again. We'd drop our surfboards and run into each other's arms. He'd tell me he should have never let me go. Then we'd drive across the country together in his orange Beetle, passing corn fields in Indiana and Cows in Texas, all the way to San Diego, California.

I was almost as addicted to the pain of missing Jimmy as I was to him. It was much more bittersweet to miss him than it was to miss my mother, which was just plain bitter. By the time I turned seventeen, my mother had been out of my life for two years. She sounded more hopeless every time I spoke to her on the phone, and it left me feeling darker and darker inside. Triggered whenever she would call me, I'd just want the conversation to end. Who was this negative, toxic person on the other line? I wanted my pixie-ballerina back. Then I'd feel ashamed and guilty for not wanting to talk to my own mother.

My fairytale fantasies with Jimmy distracted me from the real pain of losing my mother to schizophrenia, and losing my father to his new life and girlfriend in Maryland. The winter was lonely and seemed to last forever. In school, I'd stare out the window and daydream that the orange Beetle would pull into the parking lot. I'd run out of the classroom, the nuns screaming behind me, "Leslie Reyes! Get back in here, you sinful wench!" I'd jump into the beetle in my plaid schoolgirl skirt, our surfboards strapped to the top, blasting the Hoodoo gurus from the cassette player. Jimmy would be my escape from my miserable suburban life.

Wondering how I would find him, I came up with an idea. After watching the movie *Desperately Seeking Susan*, starring Madonna, I sent a letter to the editor at *Surfing* magazine and hoped they would print it.

It read, "*Desperately Seeking Krazinski*: Jimmy in the Orange Beetle, East Atlantic was calling your name yesterday. Where were you? I miss you.*" [*Not his real name.]

I didn't sign it, or type it, or explain what it meant. I just scribbled it on a piece of scrap paper, put it in an envelope, and prayed, "If Jimmy in the orange Beetle is really my soul-mate, help me find him. Amen."

I didn't really believe that *Surfing* magazine would print my letter, since it didn't make sense to anyone but me. But, to my surprise, as well as my small circle of girlfriends' surprise, they actually published it. In the June 1988 issue of *Surfing* magazine, my love letter to Jimmy in the orange Beetle was forever immortalized in the Letters to the Editor section, with a comment from the editor which read, "*A cryptic message between two Russian Spies? Or the mating call of two young New Jerseyites?"* (If you can find a copy of the June 1988 issue of *Surfing* magazine, you will get to see my note, as well as Jimmy's real name. I saw one on eBay going for $225. Sure wish I'd kept my copy.)

And that was that! The angels had spoken. Jimmy and I were meant to be. Yet I was no closer to finding him. In reality, I didn't think I'd ever bump into him again. I figured he was out of New Jersey and off at San Diego State University on a surfing scholarship or something. So I put my thoughts of Jimmy on the shelf and focused on trying to get my driver's license.

After failing the DMV road test on my seventeenth birthday, I eventually got my driver's license on the second try, just as summer was starting to pick up. My dad did not buy me a brand-new white Volkswagen Cabriolet, but I was perfectly grateful for my seafoam-green 1981 Honda Accord. I wasted no time covering the windows with stickers representing various brands of surfboards, wetsuits, and surfboard wax. My car was screaming, "Surfer girl obsessed with surfer boys on board!" to make it easy for Jimmy to find me. As soon as my dad gave me permission to drive on the highway, the Garden State Parkway became my second home, and I'd drive down to Long Beach Island on my days off of work from my part-time job at Paramus Park Mall. One hundred Parkway exits later, past East Atlantic Avenue in Harvey Cedars, I'd check the beach to see if Jimmy was surfing there every weekend. There was never any sign of him. He must have made it to San Diego.

And then one day, it happened. It went down the way I imagined it, too. Almost. Well, not exactly. So, instead of passing each other on the dunes on East Atlantic Avenue, with surfboards under our arms, I was in my green Accord pulling into Faria's Surf Shop with my girlfriends. An orange Beetle covered in surfing stickers was coming in the opposite direction, and I screamed, "Omigod! It's the orange Beetle!" My girlfriends started screaming along with me, as if it were 1964 and we were watching Ringo, Paul, George, and John performing as the Beatles on the Ed Sullivan show for the first time. Frantically waving our arms at the orange Beetle to pull into Faria's Surf Shop parking lot, we jumped out of our cars as soon as we came to a stop.

"Leslie in the green Accord. Did you write that letter to me?"

"Oh my god, you read it?"

"Uh, yeah, every surfer in the United States read it."

I was floating on a cloud. I found him. My fairytale was about to begin.

Jimmy invited me to a party in Surf City that night. There were stars in my eyes. He wrote the address on my hand. Said to be there by 8 p.m. When my girlfriends and I showed up, we were like mini-celebrities amongst the local surfers.

"So, you're the girl who wrote that letter in *Surfing* magazine?" they'd ask me.

"Did you know that Jimmy went driving up and down every street in Beach Haven looking for you after that was published?" Morty told me.

I asked Jimmy to the prom. He said yes.

A couple weeks before the prom, he chickened out and told me he couldn't go. I ended up taking a platonic friend of a friend to the prom. It was totally uneventful.

Back in Long Beach Island a few weeks later, Butch told me there had been a little bit of drama regarding my prom invitation.

"Jimmy had an anxiety attack thinking about hanging out with all the rich kids in North Jersey. I know he acted all cool when he canceled on you, but he got himself all nervous and panicked. I told Jimmy he would regret not going to the prom with you. Up in North Jersey where everyone is rich and taking a limo into New York City? I told him I wanted to go with you. I've never been in a limo or to New York. Then he got all pissed off at me."

Yes, Jimmy was supposed to be my soulmate. But he was only eighteen years old. I was seventeen years old and had a curfew. After a party one night, he slept with another girl and inevitably got her pregnant. I was a virgin when I met him. I'd wanted him to be my first. I planned it all out one hot summer night. I bought condoms at the same 7-11 where our fated paths had crossed, and invited him over to the rickety apartment that my parents had rented me and my girlfriends for the week. I kicked my friends out of the apartment at 6:30 and told them not to come back until after 10 p.m. Over an hour later than I had expected to see him, Jimmy finally showed up. I put my favorite "Dancing Hoods" album into my cassette player and confessed my love to Jimmy, telling him I wanted him to be my first.

"I can't do this, this is crazy!" he said, jumping out of my bed. He turned me down. I was crushed. He said he couldn't because he cared about me too much. Then put his shirt back on, and walked down the stairs of the wooden deck to his car. I stood at the top of the deck, and just watched him. He stopped before he got into his car, turned around. We stood there, looking at each other for what seemed like an eternity but was probably only about a minute. I kept hoping he would say something to make it all better, or change his mind and come back upstairs and hold me.

"Come back, Jimmy," I begged as a tear rolled down my cheek.

Instead, he just said, "I'm really sorry. I can't see you anymore." And drove away.

I was utterly confused, and heartbroken. My friends came home after midnight, and chastised me for being such a sucker over a boy. Needing answers, a few days later, I rode my bicycle to Butch's house and complained about it. Knowing that Butch could not keep a secret to save his life, I got him to spill the beans on why Jimmy dumped me when I tried to lose my virginity to him.

"I don't know nothing!" That's exactly what Butch would say when he knew everything.

After much haranguing, Butch finally confessed, "The reason Jimmy broke up with you, is because he's got a problem that could potentially last nine months." I knew exactly what he meant, and I was crushed.

"Jimmy really does care about you, Leslie. He's just a stupid eighteen-year-old dude, though." Butch said to try to console me.

Winter 1989

After my summer with Jimmy ended and I'd gone off to college, Jimmy started seeing someone who was living in the same dorm building as me. So he and Morty would show up in the middle of the night and try to get Sherri and me to hang out with them. Sherri was already dating someone else at the time (though Morty would soon convince her to dump the poor guy). Sometimes, the guys would show up in the middle of the night and we'd be too annoyed and tired to open up the door for them. So either Butch, Jimmy, or Morty would pull the fire alarm, and all the girls from the dorm would run outside in various states of disarray. Some would be wearing T-shirts and boxers, others little see-through baby-doll nighties or their college sweatshirts and fuzzy slippers, another in nothing but a towel because she'd been showering at the time of the alarm.

I'd use these opportunities to berate Jimmy for cheating on me every chance I got.

Looking back as an adult, I have the utmost respect for Jimmy for turning me down. He was an eighteen-year-old horndog, and he knew that I loved him, and he didn't want to take away something so special from me. And even though he didn't want to say goodbye to me, he did it anyway, and that's pretty respectful for an eighteen-year-old dude.

I can't say that about the guy who actually took my virginity. And when I say "took," I mean took.

One weekend Sherri was going home to be with her family. She lived about twenty-five minutes away from campus in Point Pleasant on the Jersey Shore. I didn't drive home on the weekends anymore. And not because it was over an hour away.

I'd driven home a couple weeks earlier because I was feeling depressed at school. I was just homesick and wanted to feel like I was with family. Unfortunately, I had totally forgotten that my father was with his girlfriend, who lived three hours away. When I came home to an empty house, I fell on my bed and cried.

So, I was preparing for another lonely weekend on campus. About forty-five minutes after she had left, Sherri came back to our dorm room and told me she wanted me to come home with her and meet her family. I was so excited. She told me to bring my surfboard. Maybe we could take turns on it. When we got to Sherri's house in Point Pleasant Beach, we found an old surfboard in her basement covered in dirt and clumpy wax. Using a hairdryer and a spatula, we removed the sand and melted surf-wax so we could see what we had. We patched up a few dings with some clear nail polish. Sherri and I were surfing soulmates.

The first time we tried to surf together, there weren't really any surf-able waves. New Jersey is not necessarily the best place to try to learn how to surf. The waves are unpredictable and change with the wind. We paddled out along the north jetty in vain, as the current pulled us down to the south jetty before we could even catch a wave. Sherri was not deterred. Instead, she happily paddled around and put all her effort into getting the hang of the sport on the small and choppy swells.

Sherri had a plan to slowly cultivate her surfing skills, even if she didn't always catch a wave. She understood how to pace herself and she lived in the present moment. She understood how to appreciate and enjoy the process of learning a new skill.

Meanwhile, I felt like surfing was just one more thing that I wasn't good at.

By the end of the semester, Sherri knew how to surf. She even won fifth place in her first surfing competition in Long Beach Island that year. On the other hand, I began to experience anxiety attacks in the water and soon, I hung up the surfboard for good.

Sherri understood something that Jaimal Yogis said in his book, *Saltwater Buddha: A Surfer's Quest to Find Zen on the Sea*:

"From the perspective of utter love for surfing, paddling was always okay, no matter how difficult, no matter how hopeless. Sure, it wasn't always as fun as riding a wave. But it was part of it. They were the same—interdependent. No paddle, no surf. No samsara, no nirvana.

"And if paddling on a day like this could be enjoyable, I figured maybe all of life's challenges could be—maybe even a real job. Maybe there was no rat race to escape."

Sherri also knew that she wanted to be a nurse. She was leaving our private university for community college and moved back home. I remember the day she decided. Another classmate of ours had decided to become a nurse, too. The two of them hugged each other and jumped up and down in excitement. "Yay! We're going to be nurses!" they laughed. I was happy for her while simultaneously feeling let down that I was going to lose my roommate. Also, I was jealous that she had a plan and I didn't. In comparison to Sherri's grounded plan of action, I had my sights set on making it big in music.

The 1970s

Music and dancing were a big part of my childhood. I always thought I'd follow in my mother's footsteps and become a ballerina. I started taking ballet lessons when I was about five. When my Uncle Pete upgraded to a Grand piano for my cousins, he gifted their old baby grand piano to me. I started taking piano lessons when I was six.

Then, when I was about nine years old, my parents took me to see the Broadway musical *Annie*. The lead role was played by a preteen Sarah Jessica Parker, a couple decades before *Sex and the City* would make her a superstar. It was then that I realized I wanted to be a singer and an actress. I memorized every song from the show. I sang along to the record with my friend Kathy, and we'd act out the different scenes from the play. Kathy's father worked as a stagehand on Broadway, *Annie* being the current show he worked on. When Kathy's parents would comment that I sounded exactly like the girls on the record, I felt validated. Kathy's dad worked on the show, after all. This was legit.

Kathy's dad had mentioned that auditions for *Annie* were being held in New York City. I begged my mother to take me. But, my father forbid it. He said if I still wanted to be a singer and an actress when I was an adult, I could pursue a career on Broadway then.

September 1989

So, here I was, finally an "adult." I was on my own, already in my sophomore year away at college. I was finally old enough to start pursuing a career in music. Where to begin, though? In the late 1980s, record companies were spending ridiculous amounts of money on new talent. But getting one of these multi-million-dollar record deals was like finding a needle in a haystack. I didn't have a backup plan to winning the rock and roll lottery.

Good at dreaming of the future, I could create positive imagery of the vision I wanted to pursue in my imagination. The problems started when I tried to envision the steps I'd need to take to get there in the real world. This was even evident during the simplest of tasks. Like when I'd try to fill out a form.

In the 1980s, when I was applying for college, the applications were paper and we had to fill them in with a pen and mail it off at the post office. There were no online computerized applications like today. Like clockwork, I'd run out of room on the lines of the application when I was filling out my name and address. I can still hear my father chastising me.

"Les, your handwriting is terrible. You keep running out of room on these applications because you are not planning ahead."

Nope. I was not in the habit of planning ahead, or even looking ahead for that matter.

What I know now is that these types of habits, even not planning ahead to make sure you have room on a form, end up making up our entire lives. My bad money habits started when I was a kid. My godfather (my Uncle Cesar) was a doctor. He would hand me ten-dollar bills starting when I was about six years old. I would always give the money to my parents for safe keeping.

They would spend it on new shoes or clothing for me. However, they left me out of the process. So, then I'd say, "Hey, you know that ten-dollar bill Uncle Cesar gave me? I want to buy this Barbie doll with it."

"Oh honey," my parents would say, "we already spent that on a new winter coat for you."

What my parents could have done was open a bank account for me. It would have been the perfect opportunity to teach me about managing money. As usual though, they were a bit distracted with my mother's mental health. After this happened a few times, I found myself immediately taking any money Uncle Cesar gave me, and spending it on something frivolous.

When I first went away to college, I brought my poor money skills with me. Wherever you go, there you are.

Banks schemed to get young people addicted to credit. They had tables set up in the college cafeteria on a regular basis. A nice-looking old man said I qualified for a credit card. Only 19.9 percent interest. It had a $500 limit. Everyone needs to start developing a good credit report, he explained. Of course, I know now what a bad deal this was.

The first thing I ever charged on my new card was taking all my friends out for nachos at Bennigan's. I also bought everyone margaritas with their fake IDs. My first credit card bill said a minimum payment of $0.00 was due. I could totally afford that. My friends and I joked that we could go shopping when we were depressed with our "free money." I probably paid for that Bennigan's meal ten times over.

Again, I had no realistic plan as to how I was going to pay these credit cards off. So I kept my focus on becoming a famous singer. If Madonna could get famous with her Minnie Mouse–sounding voice, singing "Like a Virgin," surely I could hit it big, too. I knew my voice was good.

September 1989

Back at college for my sophomore year, things were looking dark for me. I was back in the dorms, feeling misunderstood by my peers. Socially, I was still having trouble relating to the other girls in my dorm. I was in a dark, lonely place without Sherri, and I missed our little off-season trips to Long Beach Island to hang out with our group of surfers.

To keep myself from isolating in my room with my guitar,

I decided to hit some fraternity parties with some of my dorm-mates. At one particular party, I ran into this guy named Dan who I'd met in the cafeteria the week earlier. Dan was cute. He looked like "the boy next door." He had short, straight sandy-brown hair and hazel eyes and said he was studying biology, hoping to become a dentist. Dan recognized me from the cafeteria at the party right away. He pumped me a beer from the keg, and then we chit-chatted for a bit about what we wanted to do with our lives once we graduated and how we both liked to surf in Long Beach Island.

After a couple beers, Dan took my hand and said, "Let's go somewhere quiet to talk."

We walked up the narrow stairs between wood-paneled walls to a room in the finished attic that had nothing in it but a mattress.

"Ummm," I said staring at the mattress, "like, just so you know, I'm a virgin and kind of want to save that act for when I'm in a relationship. So, like, we can do other stuff, but I don't want to have actual sex."

"Okay, that's cool," he said quickly before pulling me onto the mattress on top of him. We were making out and nothing seemed out of the ordinary, when he rolled on top of me and pulled my pants off so fast.

"Wait…" I gasped, but before I knew what was happening, he was inside of me.

"Stop! I have to go to the bathroom," I said, to keep him from going any further.

"Seriously, right now?" he complained.

It was too late. I noticed I was bleeding and started crying.

"Why did you do that?" I sobbed. "I told you I was saving myself for someone special!" I pulled my pants back on and curled up on the mattress in the fetal position and started crying uncontrollably. I felt so humiliated and stupid for trusting him.

"Shit, shit." Dan panicked as he zipped up his pants. "It's okay, let's just get out of here."

"No. I don't want to go back out there," I said flatly. "Just leave me alone."

"Come on, please? We can't stay in here. Just please…let's go?" Dan pleaded, pulling at one of my arms, while I lay limp and curled up on the mattress.

After a few minutes, my tears ran dry and I just stared at the wood-paneled walls. Dan was frantic, but I couldn't hear anything he was saying to me. I was stunned I'd been betrayed and violated by someone I'd had a crush on, and now I couldn't speak or move. He finally gave up on me and left the room. Paralyzed in the dark, I don't know how long I was in there alone. Eventually a couple of my girlfriends found me still curled in the fetal position and took me home. First, they tried to console me by saying, "That fucking asshole! This was NOT your fault, Leslie." Followed by, "Next time, though, don't go off alone and drunk with some random guy." I hadn't been drunk though. And I'd been really clear about what I did and didn't want to do with him on that mattress. And he wasn't just "some random guy." He was Dan, the biology major I'd had a crush on, who I'd met in the cafeteria, who wanted to be a dentist someday and liked to surf in Long Beach Island.

Back at the dorm, I tried to sleep. I made a conscious decision not to take a shower or throw my clothes away. I'd read that's what girls would do when they are raped, and I didn't want to admit I'd been raped.

While I was curled up in my bed still wearing the outfit I'd worn to the party (an oversized sweater with rainbow stripes and a pair of baggy jeans), the fire alarm went off. I ran outside hoping it was Morty, Butch, and Jimmy playing another prank. To my dismay, it had been an actual fire. Someone hadn't snuffed out their cigarette completely before throwing it in the trash.

When I became more and more depressed after the incident with Dan, one of my friends encouraged me to start seeing a therapist. When I told my therapist what happened with Dan, she was distressed. She believed me, then reluctantly said that she didn't think it was a good idea for my mental health to report him. Not because she didn't believe I'd been raped, but because she believed no one else would.

"You will have to relive that moment over and over. They will try to discredit you and will drag you through the mud. You will feel like you are just being raped over and over again. And, most likely, he will just get off."

I knew she was right, and that pissed me off. At the same time, I felt relieved. I just wanted to move past it. Forget it ever happened.

But I could never forget. There would be no justice or closure in this situation for anyone. There was no way I could protect any other girls from him, either. My trust in myself had been lost. Already afraid to make any decisions on my own, I became more insecure after this event and it had a negative effect on many of my relationships in the future.

By the way, Dan (not his real name) is now a dentist in New Jersey.

After that, I stopped hanging out with the girls who liked to go to frat parties.

One day I was doing my laundry in the basement of the art studio, and three guys had a drum set and some amplifiers set up and were jamming. They had been band geeks in high school, and were now funneling their musical talent into rock and roll. They let me sing "Hit Me with Your Best Shot" by Pat Benatar and "Love Removal Machine" by the Cult with them one afternoon while I was washing my clothes. They hated fraternity boys and just wanted to play music. They invited me to sing with them every week and gave me a list of songs to learn to sing, which included a couple of Bon Jovi songs, Motley Crue, and a Sammy Hagar–era Van Halen song. Although not a fan of this particular genre of music, I didn't care because I was so damn happy to be singing.

I found solace from the pain I was experiencing at college through singing. I wasn't thinking about boys, or rejection, or loneliness, or how much I missed Sherri when I was singing. I could sing words that were otherwise too awkward to say out loud, that described perfectly what I'd been going through emotionally.

My friend Mike was a music major and had played in a local band called Phoenix when he was in high school. He told me about this newspaper in New Jersey called *EC Rocker* (previously *The Aquarian*). I could run free ads in it to look for band members. Or, I'd search the classifieds for bands looking for a singer. Finding the right band was harder than I thought it would be.

It was the late 1980s and I wanted to be the next Susanna Hoffs from the Bangles. But every band I auditioned for wanted me to look like a hooker with Jon Bon Jovi's hair. After all, this was New Jersey.

Right in the middle of 1980s New Jersey hair band central, I didn't relate to the soulless corporate rock that was being fed to us over the airwaves. Feeling like I had been born a generation too late, I was jealous of my baby boomer parents who had grown up with the Beatles, Jimi Hendrix, and the Allman Brothers. My favorite singer was Ann Wilson from Heart, and I loved their Led Zeppelin–influenced style. Preferring the rough-around-the-edges power-pop garage-band sound, like the Smithereens and Big Star, I was always disappointed when I'd find that the bands I was auditioning for wanted a bleached-blonde, big-boobed Lita Ford.

Then, later that semester, it finally happened. To the dismay of the boys in the laundry room who had hoped someday we'd play out as a cover band in the student recreation center, I joined my first real band. Answering an ad for a female singer in the *EC Rocker* classifieds, I met some girls in a

South Jersey band whose singer had recently quit to finish college. Heavily influenced by the bands of the British invasion, like the Yardbirds and the Kinks, they had named themselves "London Underground."

Yes. An all-girl band. My fantasy of growing up to be the next Susanna Hoffs was coming true. We even had a manager representing us, and he was paying for all our rehearsal studio time, publicity photos, and recordings. The other girls in the band were trying to sound like the Rolling Stones meet the Hollies. But we really did sound more like the Bangles or the Go-Go's, which was fine with me. Everyone in the band was between the ages of eighteen and twenty years old. In all honesty, we all looked about fourteen or fifteen. We had to go into the East Village of New York City one weekend to get fake IDs so we could play at the bars down the shore.

Within a couple of weeks of rehearsing, we were playing out at little clubs in Asbury Park. Some guys sitting at the bar of the T-Bird's Cafe watched us four short little women as we set up on stage. One of them laughed, "How old is this band? Like, nine?"

Then we played, and we were good. The four of us harmonized effortlessly, the rhythm section was tight, and our guitarist could play along with the best of the boys in the Jersey music scene.

At the time, I didn't have any professional vocal training. And I hadn't changed my college major to music yet. So, by the time we finished recording our demo, practicing two nights a week and playing at least one gig a month, I started losing my voice and I was freaking out. I'd finally found the one thing I felt like I was good at. Maybe I would win the rock and roll lottery after all. But I couldn't do that if I was going to lose my voice. I had no singing technique.

That's when my anxiety led me to an unhealthy relationship with a vocal teacher.

When I spoke to her on the phone about losing my voice,

she described very clearly how she could help me. Compared to other voice teachers I'd spoken to, she really seemed to know her stuff when it came to vocal technique. And she was so passionate about it. She advised me not to sing or rehearse for two weeks and just rest my voice. We didn't have any gigs scheduled at the time, so it was good timing. I let my bandmates and our manager know, and they were initially fine with letting me rest my voice for two weeks until I could learn vocal techniques.

That is until, a few days later, a last-minute slot opened up at the Stone Pony in Asbury Park. It was Bruce Springsteen's old stomping grounds and our manager wanted us to play there. Being that I was only eighteen years old and still didn't know how to speak up for myself or make decisions for myself, somehow, my new voice teacher and my band's manager were battling it out on the phone over me.

He was yelling at her, saying, "If I lose money because of you, you are going to get sued!"

"Go ahead and sue me!" my voice teacher said. "I'm looking out for this young lady's voice and her best interests!"

My voice teacher said to me, "You have an amazing singing voice. That band would be nothing without you. Do not let them just use you up just to toss you aside for a new singer when you lose your voice. Think long-term here and take care of number one. You are number one."

I suddenly felt so safe and protected. The most protected and safe I'd ever felt since before my mother's miscarriages. This woman was looking out for my best interests. I trusted her with all my heart after she stood up to my band's manager that way.

I ended up quitting that band, because, like my voice teacher had pointed out, if I lose my voice, they will just toss me aside and find a new singer. They were already starting to push me too hard and the effects of it were clear when I could no longer reach the notes I could sing with ease earlier that summer.

My voice teacher had lost one of her children to cancer several years before I met her. She was obviously still suffering from the loss. I mean, does a parent ever get over losing a child? It's never supposed to be that way. Her grief was as palpable as mine was for my mother. My mother was still alive, but her soul was gone.

When I told my new voice teacher about my mother's mental illness, she grew emotional. The first time I sang for her, I sang a song called "Johnny Moon" by Heart and she cried. She said she could feel the pain I'd been through in my voice.

She also said I looked like I could've been her daughter. We had the same colored hair, similar eyes, and the same small stature. She would say, "You look more like my daughter than my own daughter does." Sometimes she'd say this in front of her own daughter, and that was awkward. Her daughter would cry, "Mom. I told you that it really hurts me when you say that."

But she would still talk that way in my private lessons. She told me she wished she could've been the mother to me that my mother couldn't be. I was eighteen years old and starving for a maternal figure.

I learned no one could take the place of a real mother.

This woman ran her voice lessons as if they were a Scientology seminar. You get an initial free consultation, there is some validity to what is being offered, and you feel a lot better after the first meeting. We voice students crammed ourselves into her living room every Monday night, like Scientology minions cramming themselves into dirty scientology dorm rooms, to either be verbally berated or put on a pedestal in front of the whole class. You never knew which one you were going to get. Then, the next thing you know, you're being gaslit into believing this is the only path to reach your full potential. You're being told, just take a few more classes, give a little more money, and it will all pay off in the end. You will get the salvation you need. Just follow the program and keep emptying your wallet. Am I talking about Scientology or my voice lessons?

I was terrified of losing my voice, and I needed this woman to save my voice. I also wished she could save my life. She really did know her shit when it came to singing technique. And she seemed to believe in me. However, she was running a business. I wanted the product she sold almost as badly as I needed her motherly approval. She would tell me how some day, I was going to be as famous as Aretha Franklin, and I ate it up.

But, when I didn't do exactly what my voice teacher thought I should, she'd turn around and tell me I was too flaky to make it in the business. She'd say, "Get your shit together. Don't expect me to put my name on you if you are going to act like a flake. You will never amount to anything like this."

I believed that too.

I had no clue how I was going to be the next Aretha Franklin. A lost girl from New Jersey aimlessly trying to put myself out there, randomly tossing fliers around, going to sketchy places to audition for god-knows-what. I had no grip on the reality of what it really took to make it in the music business. I was a dreamer. Marketing and selling myself required more planning.

I didn't know my worth or my true value back then. Even on a minimum wage salary, I wanted to take a forty-five-minute voice lesson from my teacher every week. She charged about $35. On top of the lessons, she expected all her students to attend weekly group classes in her living room every Monday night for three hours, and once a month on Tuesdays for two more hours. That was going to run closer to $109.00 a week, which was going to be difficult on my paltry part-time income of about $4.10 an hour.

And she only accepted cash.

Sometimes, I'd need to take a week off from lessons when I'd realize I was using my "free money credit card" a bit too much. I'd tell her I was running short on funds, and that I needed to catch up on my finances. She would guilt trip the fuck out of me. She would tell me that if I really wanted to be a famous singer someday, I'd figure out a way to pay her. Or she'd let me take lessons on credit, racking up a debt with her.

"Someday, you are going to be a rich and famous singer, and you can pay me back then," she'd say. "Stop being a flake."

Occasionally, I might show up to class in a new shirt. I'd find something for $10 off the discount rack at Nordstrom and buy stage outfits or clothes for work or school.

Using my credit card, of course, because my voice teacher was getting all my cash.

If I'd show up wearing a new shirt, shoes, bracelet, anything…she'd say she felt disrespected. Because I was buying clothes at the mall instead of paying her off first.

But of course, she didn't accept credit cards.

I was waiting tables and giving her all my cash while going to college. I put the rest of my life (gasoline, groceries, stage wear, microphones, recording equipment, sheet music, CDs, etc.) on my credit card. I decided not to worry about it. "Someday I will be a millionaire," I told myself.

Pursuing my music career in a similar fashion to the way I lived the rest of my life, I ignored my own well-being. I did not set any personal boundaries in place. The constant sacrifices revealed my desperation for approval. I told myself over and over again that I would not use my credit cards anymore, but I always did. The irony of it was that at the time, I thought I wanted a career in music so badly. Yet I was unable to do that, because I was stuck in this voice teacher's living room. Having left any faith in myself in the attic of the fraternity house that fateful night, I was afraid to make my own decisions without her advice, while I was giving her all my money. She expected me to be at class every Monday. So I was stuck in New Jersey, too.

I believed I was making an investment in myself. I believed it would all pay off later. I just didn't know how.

With no real business plan for how I was going to become rich and famous, I thought I just needed to be the best singer I could be. The truth was, I had zero skills when it came to "selling myself." Trying to be in a successful band is like starting your own business. I had no idea how to run a business.

Also, I was terrible on stage when I tried to talk to the crowd. I couldn't read the room. I'd get so nervous, I would say dumb shit on stage and piss the other band members off.

Over the next six years, I sang in all different situations. I sang in wedding bands, a 1980s cover band, original bands where we wrote our own music. I tried out for Broadway musicals in New York City. I wanted to be in *Miss Saigon*. I got a talent agent who got me a few good jobs, and I was even in a skit with Adam Sandler and David Duchovny (that never aired, sadly) on *Saturday Night Live*. I was the understudy for Lady Thiang in *The King and I* in Roanoke, Virginia and played the lead role in *Pocahontas* in Bridgeport, Connecticut. However, my real dream was to write my own music and sing with a band.

Embarrassingly, while trying to pursue a career in music, I'd spent a lot of money on different "get rich quick" schemes when I was a starving artist. I thought that if I took this one class/seminar/workshop, then getting rich would be easy. Some of these schemes included selling candles, slinging Mary Kay, pushing Avon, peddling essential oils, and promoting vitamins. I even took a class and made a tape hoping to do voiceovers for commercials.

Still, riches eluded me.

That's because I'd always been attached to the outcome,

and not the process. When we focus on the process, that's when everything else starts to fall into place.

New Jersey, Summer 1996

After more than six years of emptying out my bank accounts and racking up my credit card debt for my voice teacher, I needed a plan to get out of those lessons. You'd think I would just quit. Just stop showing up. Why did I feel I couldn't do this? First, I never trusted my own decisions. I wanted everyone else to make decisions for me. That was the first hurdle. Second of all, I was intimidated by her. Every time I'd try to tell her it was time for me to stop taking voice lessons, she would be downright verbally abusive to me in front of the rest of the students. With my self-esteem already in the toilet by this time in my life, I'd decided I'd had enough of her calling me a flake and holding her voice lessons over my head. In pure codependent fashion, rather than set my boundaries with her and call her out over the verbal abuse, I made up a story that I needed to move to Arkansas to help my schizophrenic mother and mailed it to her so I could disappear like a coward and not hold her accountable for anything.

Pretty much everyone has the same general goals of "I want to make a lot of money, have a career I love, and retire with lots of cash." So, if everyone has the same goal, why isn't everyone a millionaire in a career they love with lots of cash when they are ready to retire?

It's because some people plan. They know how to take the necessary steps to meet their goals. They embrace the process and the steps to get there.

If we are only looking at the outcome, then we aren't living in the present. We take for granted, and even lose, precious moments in life when we do this. Planning for the future is not living in the future. Earlier in life, I had a lot of trouble distinguishing between the two. Planning means we are taking care of ourselves in case of the unforeseen. It doesn't mean to rely on something else to happen in the future to bail you out of the present.

Kind of like those crazy interest-only mortgages in the mid-2000s. The idea was that these people would only pay the interest on the mortgage the first couple years. Then they would start paying off the mortgage later. The assumption was that one would be making more money by then. It rarely worked out like that.

I paid for voice lessons with money I was hoping to make some day after I got rich and famous. This isn't living in the future as much as it is stealing from the future. Planning for the future is not to count on the future. Planning is taking care of our future selves. Not stealing from our future selves. The only moment that is real is the moment we have now.

When I get on a motorcycle, I am not planning on getting in an accident when I wear protective gear. I'm not planning on hitting my head when I wear a helmet. My protective riding gear is essential, but it doesn't mean I'm constantly thinking about how I don't want to get in an accident. All the gear, all the time. By wearing my gear, I am prepared so that I can forget about it and instead, focus on riding safely.

There are so many little things I didn't realize I had to plan ahead for when I first started riding a motorcycle. For example, if you park your motorcycle facing downhill, will you be able to get it off the kickstand? Will you be able to back it out, up an incline? It's why I look ahead when I'm on my motorcycle. I plan for how I will stop. I plan how I will put my foot down. I look to see if there is anything on the ground, like gravel or a pot-hole, which I need to be prepared for.

The first time I dropped my motorcycle, it was because I was not prepared to stop. I grabbed the brakes too hard.

"Grab is a dirty word on a motorcycle," my instructor at the Motorcycle Safety Foundation Course had told us.

This led me to hit the throttle. Followed by the 78 ft. lbs. of torque [the amount of power behind the motorcycle] slamming me and my 350-pound bike into the ground. I told myself that I needed to get into the habit of planning ahead when I was trying to brake. I figured I could start by being more mindful when I was driving in my car. Most of these things, motorcyclists end up learning the hard way.

I hate learning things the hard way.

Like my singing career. I loved the therapeutic aspects of singing. How the words I could sing in a song would have sounded awkward when spoken in a conversation. In a song, however, I could say exactly what I wanted to say in the most over-the-top fashion. People appreciated my words in the context of singing. But that's only 10 percent of it. Later, I realized, being a singer was not so much about singing. I learned the hard way, it is 90 percent about being a cutthroat business, and there are vultures out there in every form, from managers to mentors.

When I was pursuing my singing career, I was taking advice from a person who was emptying my wallet. Living in the future, instead of planning for it, was how I pursued my career. My voice teacher would tell me if I had a backup plan to my singing career, I would fall back on it. She said that if I believed in myself, I would have a career as a famous singer. I shouldn't need anything to fall back on. The problem with this plan, was that I didn't believe in myself at all. It wasn't even realistic advice to begin with. Things happen in life that we don't always plan for. Things happen that we can't always control. We also grow and change in our lives, and our dreams of the future and values change.

I'm not sure I ever wanted what it entails to be a celebrity. Sure, I was in love with the dream of being a singer. But did I really want to be the next Christina Aguilera? Tabloids, gossip, industry vampires, shit-talking predators. It never seemed like a very healthy environment.

I didn't need a backup plan in case I didn't become a famous singer. What I needed was a backup plan in case I decided a singing career wasn't for me. What I needed was a backup plan so that I would not end up beholden to someone else's agenda. Not having a backup plan is one way to lose your autonomy.

I love to sing. I don't love the music industry.

In the early 2000s, celebrities like Britney Spears and Lindsay Lohan were being treated like shit. I did not want any part of that. I didn't want to compete with Britney Spears for the spotlight. Or the bullying. Or to have my nervous breakdown in public. No thank you.

These days, Britney Spears has been in the spotlight over a conservatorship gone wrong. Basically, working like a slave to make her "caretakers" rich. I couldn't have been happier with my choice to avoid the music industry in the early 2000s. I am grateful that I got to have my mental breakdown in private. I am grateful I never sold my soul to Hollywood.

My only regret was that I did not trust myself to make my own decisions sooner.

June 2021

Part of planning ahead on a motorcycle is spending time working on our slow skills in a parking lot. This way we aren't caught off guard when someone driving a car on the road does something unexpected. Are you comfortable swerving out of the way of danger? Have you practiced smooth braking skills using the back brake, and not just the front brake?

When people who don't ride motorcycles find out that you ride a motorcycle, the first thing they do is tell you how dangerous it is, often accompanied by a "I know someone who knows someone that rides a motorcycle…" followed by some gruesome story of death.

When I am riding my motorcycle, I am not thinking about accidents or death, though. I'm focused on what is happening in front of me. Because, if I've planned ahead, by making sure my bike is safe and running properly, that my gear is protective and appropriate, and that I've chosen the route I'm going to take in advance, then I'm not going to be distracted by my own thoughts or fears. I spent eight months of weekends practicing slow skills, emergency braking, and tight turns. I made sure I was fully prepared to go on the road, before I went on the road. I did everything I could to protect my future self on the road in advance.

So, when you're thinking and planning ahead, be kind to your future self by protecting your present self.

Because it's not really a matter of IF you will encounter the unexpected, but WHEN.

When we don't plan, we steal from our future selves. It always starts small. And is barely noticeable at first.

I had stolen from my future self. Many times. It would take years for those decisions to catch up with me.

But they did eventually catch up with me, and it wasn't pretty.

4

ZEN MOTORCYCLE HABIT #4

IF YOU BREAK SOMETHING, FIX IT

"But lotuses grow from mud—and from brokenness, in my experience, beautiful things emerge. We are forced out of necessity to write a poem or song in tears. We're forced to go on retreat, into silence, into the realization that this feeble body and brain can't do it all."

— JAIMAL YOGIS, SALTWATER BUDDHA: A SURFER'S QUEST TO FIND ZEN ON THE SEA

How I loved "broken people" so I could learn to love my broken self

I was a broken Gen-X girl.

For some reason, I kept falling for guys with substance abuse issues. Which was weird, because I didn't do drugs myself.

I didn't think of myself as an addict. After all, I'd grown up in the 1980s when all the kids were listening to Nancy Reagan telling us to "Just Say No." I was never a compulsive consumer of alcohol, shopping, cocaine, food, drugs, or pills. Instead, I was addicted to romance. I was codependent as hell.

Growing up Gen-X, our Baby Boomer mothers assured us that the women's movement was won. We were now free to do whatever we wanted to do in life. We could have a career, a husband, a house, and children if we wanted them. There also seemed to be a formula for creating the perfect family life. The problem was, I didn't know if that formula was right for me.

There always seemed to be a mixed message hidden in there.

Yes, we were free to do whatever we wanted to, but we also needed to be mindful of our biological clocks. We needed to have kids first. We'd regret not having kids if we waited too long, so we were told. It was only after the husband and kids, THEN we could pursue our dreams.

However, you can't have kids with just anyone. You didn't want your kids growing up in a single-parent household. You didn't want your kids to have a shitty dad. So your husband had to be the right kind of guy. He had to have a job, be smart, and make plenty of dough. Whether or not you were compatible with said future husband never really came into play. What was important was that he checked off all the boxes, so that we women could stay home and raise the kids. Because my generation, Gen-X, had been latchkey kids, we didn't want to be the kind of parents that left their kids alone. So it was important to do all this first.

After all this, and only when these conditions were met, THEN we could pursue our own dreams. Sadly, those of us who later found out that we couldn't get pregnant, never had our dreams addressed. Had I known being a mother was not in the cards for me, I may have done things in my life a little differently.

Still, I didn't dream of what my wedding dress would look like when I was growing up. Instead, my dream was to find a husband who also dreamed of a life making music. I dreamed of what the dress I'd wear to the Grammy's would look like.

Instead of dreaming of walking down the aisle of a church on my father's arm, I dreamt of walking up on stage with my musical soulmate to accept our awards. Like Pat Benatar and Neil Giraldo. Like Debbie Harry and Chris Stein. Like Gwen Stefani and Tony Kanal. Rather than a flowing mermaid-style wedding gown of satin and lace, I imagined myself in a tight purple bejeweled number I'd seen at a formalwear dress shop at the Garden State Plaza shopping mall in Paramus, New Jersey. Picture what a Vegas showgirl would don on stage to perform high kicks as she exuded campy glamour, with a dash of Jersey.

When it came to relationships, I often wished there was a book that would fall from the sky and land in my hands. This magical book would tell me who my soulmate was and exactly when I would meet him. It would also include an instruction manual so that I wouldn't do anything "wrong" to scare my soulmate away.

Courtship was confusing. My dad would tell me, if a guy really liked me, he would find a way to get in touch with me. Our number was in the phone book, he reminded me. As a result, I wondered if a guy I was dating didn't call me every day, should I be mad about it?

Like when John Cusack holds up the radio outside of Ione Skye's window in the movie *Say Anything*. We all bought it. The epitome of romance. I thought that if a guy was interested in me, he should blast Peter Gabriel's "In Your Eyes" outside of my bedroom window and fight for my love! In reality, this is stalking. John Cusack was not respecting Ione Skye's boundaries at all.

I also received a message from somewhere, that to win a guy's heart, I had to put up and shut up. Just be the cool girl. Make him think you can live without him. Play a bunch of games that will manipulate him into thinking he can't live without you. But don't let him know who you really are right away.

In the 1990s, there was a best-selling book called *The Rules* that all the single women in their twenties were reading. It was basically a book about how to manipulate a man into marrying you. It was all very toxic and counter-productive. Ultimately, this just leads to ending up in a relationship with people who aren't right for us.

"False advertisement" is what the drummer in my California band, Matty, would call this.

June 1999

I realized I was running out of time to do all the above. The year 2000 was looming like the coming of an apocalypse. Already in my late twenties, I was beginning to feel like my last chance to pursue a singing career was looming around the corner. On top of that, my biological clock was ticking. I needed a hit album before I could get married and have babies. With no luck finding the right husband who would ride off into the rock and roll sunset with me, or a record deal in New Jersey (or Manhattan), I didn't want to live with my dad in Mahwah, New Jersey forever. However, getting an apartment in New Jersey didn't make sense when I was already living in New Jersey for free.

If I was going to move out, I was *really* going to move out.

I thought about moving to Manhattan, right over the George Washington Bridge. But, then I realized Los Angeles was literally half the price of New York City at the time. There were beaches there. The weather was perfect and I could keep my car. So I started saving half of my paycheck from my medical transcription job by automatically depositing it into a savings account.

I still needed a demo of my singing, though.

After much begging and pleading, I got a group of musician friends together. They helped me record a demo of a couple of songs I'd written. I had about 100 CDs pressed (paid for on my credit card). I decided to bring these CDs to California with me and try my luck in Hollywood.

Somehow, I had managed to save enough money to move to Los Angeles. I packed up my car, and my friend Kris joined me on a ten-day cross-country journey from our homes in New Jersey. With my silver Honda Civic packed to the brim, I asked Kris if she was okay in her seat. She said, "Sure, if I get tired, I'll just put the seat like…"

She made an attempt at reclining the seat—It didn't budge.

"I'll just leave the seat like this," she surrendered.

Our first overnight stop was at a friend of Kris's who lived in Knoxville, Tennessee. A girl she had gone to high school with was living there and we had lunch with her and napped in her living room. Then we drove to Memphis and had dinner and drinks on Beale Street. We stayed in a shady motel surrounded by stray kittens. Kris was an animal rescuer. She stayed up half the night feeding the kittens cat food she bought from the 7-11 across the street.

When we got to Arkansas, I wanted to get in touch with my mother. She was living there but I had no idea what state of mind she was in. Would she be clear, or would she be smack dab in the middle of a psychotic episode? I called her from a payphone in a park in Little Rock, but she didn't answer. The wind was whipping around me and I started to cry. Kris said, "Maybe it's too much right now. You're making a huge life change. You're moving out of your dad's house and all the way to the other side of the country. Maybe you should try to contact your mom once you get settled."

I knew she was right. I just wanted my mommy at that moment. Kris had so many friends and family members embracing her as we drove across the country. I was starting to feel like an orphan. I wanted to see my mom and make cookies with her and go shopping with her like old times. None of that was going to happen right now.

So we left Arkansas and drove to Oklahoma. We visited Kris's step-sister who was living there. She and her boyfriend took us up to a wide open park on a hill where wild Buffalo roamed. There was a beautiful old chapel in the middle of the prairie where murals of the Virgin Mary were painted on the ceiling. Back in the car, Texas seemed to stretch on forever and ever. I looked over at Kris, who had taken her pillow and placed it on the dashboard and was sleeping slumped forward. When she woke up, she took one look outside the window, dazed, and asked, "Where the hell are we?" Nothing but oil rigs dotted otherwise empty plains. She then realized that the Freon from the car's air-conditioner had infused her pillow with a peculiar scent, which she complained about the rest of the trip.

"Dammit, my pillow smells like dirty feet!" she exclaimed, exasperated.

We ended up staying in a motel near Lubbock. The linens were not much fresher in the motel than they were in my car. In the morning at the café, families stared at Kris's bare midriff and my tattoos before they bowed their heads in prayer to say grace. We arrived in Roswell, New Mexico on a Sunday night. Just in time to watch *The X-Files* on television. Roswell is famous for what many believed to be a UFO crash and a government conspiracy. I had what I thought was a mosquito bite on my chest and made a joke that I had caught an alien virus in Roswell.

When we got to the Grand Canyon, I wasn't feeling right. I was extremely lethargic and didn't feel up for hiking. We took some photos of the beautiful gold, red, and sienna canyon with brushstrokes of lavender shadows, and then found a hotel in Flagstaff. The next morning we headed to Sedona. The road there was windy and lined with gorgeous pine trees and mountains. Every corner we turned, the vistas became more and more beautiful. As we headed south, the terrain changed from lush green trees against a cerulean blue sky, to desert orange against a violet sunset. We had dinner at a Mexican Restaurant in Sedona and stayed in an amazing Southwestern spa-style hotel.

The next morning I woke up covered in little white, vaguely visible spots.

"What does chicken pox look like?" I asked Kris.

"Didn't you have that as a kid?" she asked.

"Nope."

"You're probably just stressed out and giving yourself a rash."

"Um, I'm not sure that I can manifest this rash just from stress."

We drove to Phoenix the next morning to visit another one of Kris's friends. By the time we got there, I was so weak I could barely lift my head. I was also feeling depressed and lonely, as I realized Kris had more friends and family all over the country than I did. Kris and her friend went out to eat and I slept on the couch. When I woke up the next morning, Kris said, "Oh my god. Don't look in the mirror."

"Why?"

"You were right. You have chicken pox."

I looked like a circus freak. I couldn't believe I was going to spend my first few weeks in Los Angeles, the capital of glamour and good looks, swollen and covered in oozing sores. I bought a half a dozen bottles of calamine lotion and poured them all over myself. I wore pajamas the rest of the drive from Phoenix to Los Angeles. Then I called my soon to be new landlord from a payphone at a truck stop in Palm Springs to let him know I'd be arriving in a couple of hours.

We arrived in Los Angeles at 8 p.m. on July 1, 1999. I was covered in spots and calamine lotion. My landlord snapped a Polaroid photo of me while I was bringing boxes into my new place and said, "You can show that to your kids someday."

I was just about living within my means when I first got to California. Luckily, it was relatively affordable in 1999. Gasoline was only $1.35 and I could buy enough groceries at Trader Joe's to last me two weeks for about $35 to $40.

I was working as a medical transcriber at Cedars-Sinai Medical Center during the day making about $17 an hour. (Sadly, the types of jobs I was doing in Los Angeles that paid $17 an hour in the 1990s, are STILL only paying $17 an hour today, more than twenty years later.) I had my nights open to pursue music.

Once I settled into my new apartment in Los Angeles, and after seeing Kris off at the airport as she headed back home to New Jersey, I started looking for a band. It didn't take long. I found a band that already had a bit of a following, and they were looking for a new singer. Their former lead singer had been a backup vocalist on one of the Red Hot Chili Peppers' albums. I loved that type of rock and roll sound with a funky edge.

I totally clicked with this band, and our songwriting together was effortless. We were rehearsing two to three times a week at night at a studio in Orange County. I believed I was destined to become a famous singer, mainly because I felt like it was the only thing I was good at.

Even though I started singing in bands when I was eighteen, somehow, I'd managed to keep myself sheltered away in my voice teacher's living room, far from the riff-raff of the rock and roll world. I was always too worried about my vocal cords to drink alcohol or caffeine. Much less smoke anything else or do drugs! I was clueless about addiction. So naïve, it completely baffled people.

Even though I was still pretty clueless about recreational drug use at the time, my bandmates did indulge sometimes. The typical stuff: cocaine, molly, speed, and pot. I wasn't a hard partier because I didn't want to screw up my vocal cords. To take care of my voice, I would go home right after every gig and breathe in some steam from the shower. My nightcap was a little chamomile tea with honey.

Acting like a rock star turned out to be a harder role to play than I imagined. I had a hard time pretending to enjoy talking to our fans at times. I'd have to scream over the loud music to have a conversation, and I didn't want to screw up my vocal chords. Deep down, I always felt like a grumpy old lady. I felt socially awkward, I'd miss a lot of social cues. So I developed this weird, awkward way of interacting with others. It was sort of an artificial friendliness that I learned from watching 1980s sit-coms. People who were friends with my mother always ended up drifting away the more depressed she grew. Afraid of being ostracized by my friends and relatives the same way, I stayed upbeat, friendly to a fault, complete with an awkward chuckle after every sentence.

This strategy worked until I was in my late twenties. Then my awkwardness and anxiety stopped being cute and eccentric. Instead, it turned into a liability that the other guys in my band found destructive to our image. Whether at a small gathering or on stage, I could not read the room. For example, I was dating a guy at the time whose father was working for Fox News, and misjudged George W. Bush's popularity while on stage in a room full of Southern California liberals. Seriously. Fans of ours thought I was stuck up when I was just terrified. Terrified of saying the wrong things. Terrified of losing my voice if I socialized too long in the loud, smoky bar. When my band members would try to broach the subject, it would hurt me to the core so badly. I'd become so embarrassed and upset, it was hard for them to talk to me. They couldn't give me any constructive criticism without crushing my spirit.

October 2001

After playing gigs around Southern California for almost two years, my band in Los Angeles was having trouble finding the right drummer. In fact, one of them quit because of my George W. Bush tangent.

The guys in my band had worked with a drummer named Matty before. They said that he was the best drummer they had ever worked with in the past. It wasn't the first time I'd heard them talk about their old drummer. They also mentioned that Matty had a problem with drugs in the past.

That was over three years ago, though. A lot can change in that amount of time.

The night Matty joined the band it was magical. It was "love at first listen," he said.

When Matty came to audition for the band, I saw the look on his face when I first opened my mouth to sing. He had stars in his eyes. If only someone would look at me that way forever. The problem was, he was going to be in my band. Dating band members was off-limits.

There was also the fact that I was engaged to someone else.

I had a long history with Trey, the brother of one of my high school friends. I was only fifteen when I met him. After moving to Los Angeles and finding out he was living down the street from my aunt in West Covina, we started dating. Pretty soon, we'd gotten engaged, and he was a great guy. He was exactly the kind of guy your family wanted you to marry. The perfect husband on paper. He was a financial consultant with an MBA from the University of Southern California. He was a republican. He believed a real man would never ask a woman to terminate an unexpected pregnancy. His parents were still married and he was close to his sister, just like those sit-com families from the 1980s.

On the other hand, I was an artsy democrat who had voted for Bill Clinton twice, and had a Bachelor of Arts in Music from a small state school in New Jersey. My parents were divorced and my dad was on his third wife. Not to mention, my mother was an institutionalized schizophrenic with demon babies in her womb. There was a sit-com that mimicked my relationship with Trey in the late 1990s called

Dharma and Greg. It was about a crystal-loving hippie chick who marries a financial guru from Wall Street after bumping into him on the Subway. If it worked in the sit-com world, maybe it could work in the real world.

Trey imagined us throwing dinner parties for rich friends and drinking martinis on a yacht. I dreamed of partying in Hollywood like a superstar at Whisky a Go Go, or touring with Lollapalooza. He dreamed of traveling the country doing seminars on investing. I dreamed of embarking on humanitarian missions around the globe with Eddie Vedder and Bono. Trey dreamed of investing in real estate and building a mansion for us someday. I dreamed of embarking on a mission with Habitat for Humanity and building homes for the homeless someday.

Trey is the one you wanted to marry. You knew he'd be a good father and provider. Yet he just wasn't the right guy for me, and I wasn't the right woman for him.

About a month before we called the wedding off, Trey asked me, "When are you going to grow up and stop playing rock star?" Was he kidding? He'd known me for a long time. He knew that having a career as a singer was my lifelong dream. His comments made me feel stupid. Like my dreams didn't matter.

"I mean, what kind of a life do you want to have?" he continued. "Do you even like the people who come to your shows?"

Our fans were blue collar, down to earth people from the suburbs of Orange County. They enjoyed beer, the outdoors, and good old-fashioned rock and roll. They weren't the kind of people that partied on a yacht. There wasn't a damn thing wrong with that!

The nail in the coffin for us should have been "The Song." I'm embarrassed to admit, it wasn't.

I'd written "The Song" for Trey. I wanted it to be the first dance at our wedding. It seemed to be everyone's favorite song when my band played shows. I poured my heart out into this song, a romantic ballad. Trey rejected it. I felt crushed. He didn't want it to be our first dance. My future brother-in-law, seeing my disappointment, said in the sincerest way, "I'll dance to that song with you, sweetie. I think it's beautiful." Instead, Trey chose this song called "Ice Cream" by Sarah McLachlan, which didn't even make sense for a wedding song. It was a song about sex, not love.

I called up Matty on my lunch break one day at work. He had officially joined our band and was learning our songs off a demo that we had recorded with our previous drummer. I wanted to get his unbiased opinion. He hadn't written these songs with us, and I wanted to know which ones were his favorites. He brought up two of our more upbeat songs. He said he really loved the guitar riff of one, and he loved the lyrics of the other.

Then he said, "But my favorite song?"

He then started gushing over "The Song" I'd written for Trey. The one Trey rejected.

Matty went on and on about "The Song." He said he loved it so much.

"Man, that song. I wish someone would write a song like that for me. It just brings me back to high school and I feel like I have a crush on someone. Like I'm falling in love for the first time again," Matty said.

He had no idea that my fiancé had rejected that song.

I held back my tears on the other end of the line.

"Oh, great! I'm glad you like that song."

OMG, I wanted to die, though.

That was how I had wanted Trey to feel about that song. And now all I wanted to do was cancel my wedding and find a guy who would appreciate my song as much as Matty did.

But, on the other hand, I didn't take these feelings seriously at the time. I figured it would pass. I had a crush on my drummer. It was just a dumb music crush, and I was clear on that. I was happy to be around someone who appreciated my songs and my singing voice, and we had an epic creative connection. The band was sounding better than ever. I had no plans to cancel my wedding to the perfect husband on paper who I'd known since high school. Not over a dumb crush on my drummer.

Plus, I just knew myself. I'd had too many fantasy fairytale daydreams in my life. Matty had that lost-soul energy, like Jimmy in the orange Beetle had. I'd always seemed to be unconsciously attracted to guys who I could turn into a "project." I had to fix the boys I loved, make them all better, nurture their broken spirits, like a once-gorgeous now-abandoned old Victorian home that fell into disarray, whose paint had chipped and foundation was cracked. In real life, I'd end up just being a nag and I knew it. I couldn't explain it, so I wrote a song about, inspired by Matty, called "What it Seems."

I have an attraction to your self-destructive side
I want to save you from your past
I could be your drug instead and make you dependent
  on me
And guard you in my sanctuary
But in reality
It's not your savior that I'd be
Just a stinging nag, you'd have to throw me off
  your back
So I'll just love you from a distance
Til I build up a resistance
To that look in your eyes
And then you'll surmise
That it's never quite what it seems
So I'll just love you in my dreams

It wasn't a love song for Matty. It was a warning to Matty.

Matty and I would sometimes get together after rehearsals and work on songs and lyrics over a buffet of Taco Bell in his minivan. At first, whenever Matty would call me up on our landline phone, Trey would joke, "Your other boyfriend is on the phone." See? It was all an innocent joke.

After a while, though, my fiancé was getting more and more insecure about it. Unsure how to ease his insecurities, I stopped hanging out with Matty outside of rehearsal and shows. We stopped chatting on the phone. We stopped working on music together, and we stopped going out for Taco Bell after our shows and rehearsals.

One morning Trey woke up after a bad dream. He said he had a dream that Matty and I were rehearsing with the band on a stage somewhere. After we finished the sound check, Matty and I started doing yoga poses and went into "happy baby" pose. We were laughing and giggling as if we were two little kids involved in an inside joke. Trey was sure the dream was a premonition. He thought I was cheating on him with Matty.

I was not sleeping with Matty, but, in all fairness to Trey at the time, we were involved in an emotional affair. I just didn't really know what an emotional affair was then. With no plans on acting on what I was feeling, the emotions crept up on us by surprise. We had a connection through the music that Trey couldn't compete with. It made him absolutely crazy. It was making me crazy too. It was making me feel like a bad person.

Matty and I did not want to ruin the integrity of the band. No matter what weird feelings we were developing for each other. We talked about it and we decided it was all an innocent crush. He was in love with my singing, and I was in love with the way he played his drums around my voice. We weren't in love, though, because that would be delusional. We weren't delusional, or so we thought.

Unfortunately, even after Matty and I stopped hanging out with each other outside of band rehearsal, it didn't help my relationship. Trey was looking at my cellphone behind my back and inspecting my computer's browser history. One night he went through my journals and freaked out. I would often write lyrics in my journals, or jot down dreams I wanted to remember. Then I'd use these journals to help me write lyrics for my songs. Trey couldn't tell which things I'd written were just dreams or poems, and thought they were all about Matty.

That should have been the end of it, but it wasn't. Another nail in the coffin for me was when I went home to New Jersey to work on our wedding plans. My future in-laws and my fiancé were controlling everything about the wedding. They were trying to convince me to buy a wedding dress that my mother and I hated.

When I first got engaged, my mom and I had a very difficult conversation. She had decided that coming to my wedding would be too much for her to handle emotionally. She was afraid to see my father and relatives after all these years, after having been institutionalized for so long.

Summer 1985

When I was fifteen years old, five years after I'd stopped her first suicide attempt, my mother overdosed on her psych meds while I was sleeping over a friend's house. She survived it, but was in a coma for two weeks. My father bought me to the hospital, even though I protested. Angry with my mother for trying to leave me again, I gave my father a hard time before he put his foot down and forced me to go to the hospital with him. Unprepared to see my mother hooked up to IVs and twitching as if she was in the middle of a perpetual nightmare, I fell into my father's arm and cried. Numbed by how emotionally overwhelming the situation was, I shut down. I just completely emotionally shut down and refused to go to the hospital again.

When she finally came to and was discharged from the

hospital, she swore to me that she hadn't been trying to commit suicide. She said she had a dream that angels were telling her to eat all the candy. The candy in her dream were her pills in real life. And she ate all the pills as the angels had instructed her. Making good on his promise to leave if she attempted suicide, which she had done in his mind, my father decided the marriage was done. Then my parents put me in the worst position. They asked me who I wanted to live with. I couldn't imagine going to Arkansas at age fifteen. Not only that, my mother did not have the mental capacity to take care of me and I knew it. So I chose to stay with my dad out of practicality more than anything. My mother bowed her head down and looked so defeated when I chose my father.

My mother then went to Arkansas to live with my grandmother. Visiting her in Arkansas in my teenage years was traumatic. She was unrecognizable. A petite, beautiful ballerina in her youth, she was now overweight and had ballooned out from her medications. Her voice was slow and her motions were sluggish. The light in her eyes had gone out. She acted helpless all the time and had lost her lighthearted demeanor and creative, bubbly edge. I felt like I was hanging out with the ghost of my mother or an echo of her memory every time I went to see her. It left me feeling lonely and resentful.

Summer and Fall 2001

My mother had not seen my father or any of our relatives at all during the time she had been in Arkansas, since 1985. No one had seen her this out of shape or sluggish either, and as a former ballerina, she was embarrassed. She was afraid the emotional weight of seeing everyone at my wedding after all these years would trigger a schizophrenic episode. Quite honestly, I was afraid of that too. I felt relieved that she had been the one to bring it up first. As sad as I was to realize this, I knew she was right. The wedding was going to be too stressful for her. And that would end up being stressful for me, too.

Still wanting to feel involved in my wedding, she asked me for one thing: All she wanted was to help me pick out my wedding dress. Then she would feel as if she was a part of my wedding. So, I flew her out to California for a week and I tried on dresses at a David's Bridal chain store in Torrance, California for her. She met my fiancé and we visited my cousin Margarita and my Aunt Hannelore in San Diego while she was in town.

She loved all the dresses I tried on. Except for one. The offending gown had a tight bodice that laced up the back. It was embroidered with little flowers and spaghetti straps, and had a huge, poufy, fluffy tulle skirt that made me look as wide as I was tall. She said, "Whichever dress you decide on, please don't buy that one!" While I didn't totally despise the dress, I knew it was not going to age well either.

After my mother flew back to Arkansas, Trey and I took a trip to New Jersey to finish up our wedding plans. At the David's Bridal located in Paramus New Jersey, my bridesmaids and I met up with my future mother-in-law and future sister-in-law. My bridesmaids were being fitted for the periwinkle dresses my sister-in-law talked me into. I had narrowed down my wedding dress choices and was getting everyone's opinions on them.

My future mother-in-law (MIL) and future sister-in-law (SIL) were absolutely in love with the poufy, fluffy, tulle dress that my mother had hated. They begged me to try it on, even after I told them there was no way I was going to buy that dress because my mother found it repulsive. They were relentless, so I finally gave in and tried it on for them "just for fun." MIL took one look at me and her eyes watered up with tears. She loved that damn poufy dress so much. SIL loved it too. The two of them stood there, looking breathless, as if we were all in some Hallmark commercial.

"Are you sure you don't want this dress?" SIL asked, with her hand on her heart. "You look amazing."

My cousin Mary Ellen was trying to back me up. She said, "Wow, that's…something. You look like you belong on top of a cake."

Still, SIL and MIL kept asking me, "Are you SURE you won't consider this dress?"

On the way home from the David's Bridal boutique, my cousin Mary Ellen sat in silence in the passenger seat. Her arms and legs were crossed. She was shaking her leg.

"Are you mad?" I asked her. "What's wrong? You seem upset?"

"I probably shouldn't say anything, but I can't help myself," Mary Ellen said sternly. "I'm furious. Your future in-laws have taken over your entire wedding. They are barely even letting you pick your own wedding gown. Even after you told them your mom hated that dress.

"They've chosen the wedding hall, the date, the band. What have you chosen? You wanted to have a morning brunch wedding on a Sunday. They talked you into dinner on Saturday. You wanted to save money by getting a D.J. Your fiancé insisted on a band.

"You've had to ask your dad for over $8,000 for a wedding you don't even want. You even wanted little black dresses for your bridesmaids, and your future sister-in-law talked you out of that, too. Are they going to try to control your life after you get married, as well?"

She had a point. My future sister-in-law had chosen our wedding hall, and honestly, I hated it. Trey and I were living in California. But his family and my father, step-mother, and half of my Filipino side of the family were living in New Jersey. His family convinced us to have the wedding in New Jersey since most of our friends and family were there. So I trusted my future sister in-law to help me choose a banquet hall. She sent me a link to the banquet hall's website and it looked nice enough over the internet.

Unfortunately, when I finally saw the banquet hall in person, I could not hold back my horror. The carpet was forest green covered in big pink flowers. Mirrors that looked like they were from the 1970s, covered with gold etchings, lined the walls of the dining room. It was dark inside, and painted wood paneling stretched along the walls of the foyer. The building itself was tucked in the middle of a dark, shaded, wooded area. My dream wedding had been to get married barefoot on the beach at sunset. Trey literally said, "I'm not getting married like some hippie on the beach. That's some tacky shit."

Meanwhile, SIL was all upset when she found out I didn't like the banquet hall she'd chosen. She felt like I hadn't appreciated all the hard work she'd put into trying to find a wedding hall for me. I was becoming less and less excited about getting married. I didn't feel like the wedding was about me at all. I was starting to get concerned that I was not going to be accepted for who I was in that family. The band, the song I'd written, telling me to grow up and stop playing rock star, the banquet hall…there were so many red flags.

I cried to John Michael, my manager from my job at Cedar-Sinai, about it. He was a great friend and one of my band's biggest fans. A gay man living in West Hollywood, sometimes he liked to dress up in drag. So, he was great at helping me pick out outfits for my shows.

He said, "Honey, are you sure you are ready to get married? Maybe you're just not ready."

"I just don't think we are right for each other," I sobbed.

"Well, I must admit," he said, "I was really shocked by your reaction when he proposed."

Trey had jumped on stage with my band while I was singing at a show in a club on Melrose Avenue in West Hollywood one night. It was in the middle of the week and hardly anyone was in the club. There were a couple on a couch in the corner who looked like they were rolling on ecstasy as they groped each other and made out all night, never once looking up at the stage. Not even while Trey was getting down on one knee and proposing to me in front of my microphone. I was taken by surprise. And I hate surprises. Not realizing he had told the other guys in the band that he was going to do this, I was freaking out. I thought for sure the guys were going to be upset about him jumping on stage and proposing like that.

I said yes, really quickly, then shooed him off the stage and sang "Move Over," a gritty, angry breakup song by Janis Joplin. Totally not the song to sing right after someone asks you to marry them. What the fuck is wrong with me? The following Monday at work, I was freaking out in John Michael's office.

"Why did I react like that? Oh.My.God. I ruined my own wedding proposal! Then I sang 'Move Over' by Janis Joplin? What the fuck?"

"Oh, honey, maybe you were just caught off guard and nervous," John Michael re-assured me as things continued to fall apart at home with Trey.

The rest of the year, I felt like I was walking on eggshells. Trey was still really insecure about Matty being in my band and asked me if the band would consider kicking him out.

"Absolutely not, Trey. I can't even believe you'd ask me that. You know how long it took us to find the right drummer."

This, of course, only made him feel more insecure, and I was feeling anxious and acting overly cautious, which only made Trey more suspicious. He continued to go through my journals and my phone logs. Then, one morning, Trey had yet another nightmare about me and Matty. I was over it. There was nothing I could do to make Trey feel secure about my love for him, because after all the mistrust and snooping, arguing and accusing, the new truth was, I didn't love Trey anymore.

And that was it. Four months before we were supposed to get married, the wedding was called off.

Summer 2002

The other guys in my band tried not to show their utter relief and joy at the news of my nuptials being cancelled. They admitted to calling Trey "Yoko Ono" behind my back. They thought he was too controlling for me. Matty and I continued to keep our distance from each other outside of rehearsals, while people around us were getting annoyed anyway. They could tell we were crushing on each other, even though we were doing our damnedest to "not go there." The emotions and the musical connection we had was apparent to everyone around us. This was also disruptive to everyone around us.

The more we tried to hide it, the more it seemed like it was pissing everyone off. I was afraid of what I was feeling for Matty. I didn't want to. I knew he had a difficult history with drugs. But he was swearing he was sober now. The guys in the band said they didn't care if he was still on drugs. If it didn't interfere with the band's agenda, and he showed up for rehearsals and shows, they were fine.

Not too long after Trey and I split up, Matty helped me move into a tiny studio apartment in Venice Beach. It came with a full-sized refrigerator, but there was no kitchen sink. We started making a list of things I needed in my apartment. I called it "Matty and Leslie's To Do List." We painted my bathroom a bright violet-blue. He installed a deadbolt on my front door.

But then I started adding romantic, fun things to "Matty and Leslie's To Do List." We were starting to admit our feelings for each other might not just be a crush. So I started adding things we hoped to do after the dust settled from my wedding being cancelled and we'd gotten the rest of the band's blessing.

Items on our to-do list included: Go surfing together in El Porto. Take a trip up to Sonoma and drink wine in a hot air balloon. Take another trip to the mountains and sit in a hot tub surrounded by snow. Live in an awesome hip studio with exposed brick walls downtown. Get married barefoot in the sand in Venice. Have a baby in a whirlpool and name her Venice, after the place we got married. Make music together and bring our baby girl on the road.

Everything was all so sweet and innocent, and so unrealistic.

So, one night, Matty and I stayed up late to finish painting my apartment. I woke up the next morning and found that my car had been keyed. I had a feeling I knew who it was.

Matty had a long-time "friend with benefits" named Camilla. She was very close to his family. They'd been friends for almost a decade. I referred to her as his girlfriend once when she was at one of our shows. She laughed and corrected me. "Matty is NOT my boyfriend." She rolled her eyes.

"She's my friend with benefits," Matty told me, one night when we were at Taco Bell.

"That sounds like a nightmare waiting to happen," I commented.

"If she's your best friend and you guys are sleeping together, why not just date each other?" I wondered.

The story Matty told me, is that he had been interested in having a relationship with Camilla when they first met. But she wasn't interested in him that way. So now, they were just friends with benefits. Camilla was adamant. Every time I referred to Matty as her boyfriend, she would insist, "He is NOT my boyfriend."

Camilla truly was a trusted friend of Matty's family. She would babysit his three-year-old niece, Giselle, and she even assisted with care for Matty's little brother, who was severely disabled by cerebral palsy and needed full supervision.

But what I didn't realize was that Camilla was addicted to

meth, too. They were both speed-freaks and they were using it together. I was the worst addict out of the three of us, in my opinion. I was addicted to Matty. Like a bona fide codependent, I had one drug of choice: Matty. I wanted to smoke, snort, and inject him every moment, not understanding that codependency and drug addiction are pretty much the same thing. I didn't realize Matty and I were about to embark on a very toxic addictive journey. Everyone else could sense it but us.

Matty adored his three-year-old niece, Giselle, and he talked about her constantly. I couldn't wait to meet her. Matty finally introduced her to me one night after our regular trip to Taco Bell.

"Hey, Giselle, this is the singer in my band. Remember the songs we were listening to? This is the girl who was singing them."

Giselle looked at me expressionless with her big dark eyes, looked at Matty, then turned to Matty's mother and burst into tears.

"Giselle! What on earth?" Matty's mother said, "I'm so sorry. She's not usually like this."

Yeah, that was awkward.

I just felt like, "Wow, is there something wrong with me that I'm not aware of?"

Giselle was only three years old, but she'd felt a disturbance in "The Force."

It wasn't just Giselle or my ex-fiancé who were freaking out about me and Matty. The other guys in my band were getting suspicious too. They had dealt with Matty's addiction before and knew what it looked like. I was comfortable in my own little la-la land. I had no clue.

I met up with my bassist and guitarist and their wives one night for drinks. I was talking to my guitarist's wife, Michelle, over cocktails. She had been saying how great my voice sounded lately. "It's because of the way Matty plays the drums," I said, with stars in my eyes. "He listens to my voice when he's playing, and I don't feel like I have to compete with him. He's the best drummer I've ever played with. He's, like, the drummer of my dreams."

It must've been written all over my face how infatuated with Matty I already was. Michelle took one look at me and said, "Oh my god. The band, Leslie. You cannot start dating Matty!"

"What are you talking about? I'm not dating Matty. I don't want to date Matty," I insisted to Michelle.

"Just be careful," she warned.

Matty and I had not started a physical relationship yet. But my band members and even their wives sensed something was up. After rehearsal one night, my guitarist pulled me aside and said, "You know, I couldn't hide how happy I was when you and Trey cancelled your wedding. He was totally wrong for you. Not to mention, I'm so happy I don't have to fly all the way to New Jersey to go to your wedding anymore. But I'm just going to say this once. I don't know what or if anything is going on, but Matty is wrong for you for the exact opposite reasons that Trey was wrong for you."

Matty continued to swear up and down to me that he wasn't using drugs. My bandmates knew better. Matty was showing up for rehearsals later and later. His performance started to suffer. I was in denial, and I believed Matty because I was clueless.

"He cares about me. He wouldn't lie to me."

"You're being an idiot," my guitarist told me.

He was right about that.

All this drama was going on while we were platonic. It was like the universe and everyone in it was afraid of Matty and me being together. For good reason. First, neither one of us was dealing with reality. Second, we were starting to mix...the way bleach and ammonia mix. The chemistry between us was palpable to anyone else in our orbit. Our chemistry together amounted to mustard gas.

So, back to my car.

It had been keyed. And it was Camilla who had done it. I guess Camilla had been lying to herself when she insisted that Matty wasn't her boyfriend. Because you don't key another woman's car over a "friend."

Camilla had been babysitting Matty's niece, Giselle, over at his parent's house. She accidentally saw "Leslie and Matty's To Do List" on Matty's desk, and lost her shit. That was the night Matty was at my apartment, and we'd been up late painting the bathroom. Camilla saw Matty's 1965 Ford Mustang parked in front of my building and she exploded. In Camilla's defense, Matty had been lying to her as much as she had been lying to herself. He was lying to me, the band, and his parents. Everyone. I just had no idea at the time. No wonder Camilla lost her mind. She saw red, and she keyed my car.

Matty and I were done tippy toeing around. Everyone had accused us of having a sexual affair. Trey, my band members, and now Matty's BFF with benefits. If we were going to get punished anyway, we might as well commit the crime.

Five months after my wedding was cancelled, against our better judgment, Matty and I started sleeping together. Something always felt off, though. Matty said he didn't think it was a good idea to tell the other guys in the band that we were dating. I agreed with him, mostly because I didn't want the guys to start acting differently towards me or Matty. I wanted to attempt to keep things separate until the storm of my wedding getting called off, and Camilla losing her shit, had blown over.

One night on the beach behind LAX airport, I burned all my memories of Trey in a bonfire with Matty. He confessed to me that he was currently on probation and he was in court-mandated drug treatment. He asked me not to tell the other guys in the band. He said he hadn't been 100 percent upfront with me. He'd only been sober for a year, not three. Then he relapsed about six months before joining the band. He had gotten caught by the police. Now in a court-mandated program to get sober, he had court dates and all kinds of other stuff going on.

"I'm scared," I admitted.

"Me too," he said.

And we should have been.

Matty and I continued to see each other, and tried to keep it on the down low. But one night I got a phone call from Camilla. At this point, I still had no idea that Camilla was struggling with her own meth addiction and was in a dark place herself. I felt sorry for her after the car-keying incident. She had left me a bunch of crazy voice mails apologizing, while sobbing profusely. She sent me a check for $1,000 to get my car fixed. I believed she really cared for Matty and that his sobriety was important to her.

"I think Matty is lying. I think he is using again," she told me.

I thought Camilla was doing me a favor. I thought, just as I believed her apology to me to be sincere, that she was trying to protect me and Matty. I believed she was sincerely worried about Matty. But then she shocked me.

"I have a confession to make ," she said. "Matty and I have been back together. He told me that you guys decided not to have a relationship because of the band. He said that you guys are just friends. Is that true?"

I suddenly became red hot with embarrassment.

"No, that's not true, Camilla. Like, not too long after you keyed my car, we started seeing each other. We still are."

"Ugh, I'm so sorry," Camilla responded, again sounding sincere. "He's playing both of us. I'm so mad."

Camilla then hatched a plan. She invited me over to her apartment. We parked my car in a parking lot about a mile from her house. Her friend Janelle was there so it wouldn't look suspicious when Matty came over. It would just seem like another Friday night at Camilla's. She called Matty and told him to come over, and then told me to hide in her bathroom.

I heard Matty walk into the house. He started talking to Camilla all casually, cracking jokes. Then I heard Camilla say, "Matty, you know, I'm still really upset about Leslie."

"Oh, come on! Not this again. Cam…"

"Are you lying to me about her? Did you guys really call it off? Because I don't want to be doing this with you anymore if you are ready to move on," Camilla insisted.

I heard Matty sigh and say, "Cam, come on! I told you. Leslie and I can't be together because of the band."

"So, you guys are not together?"

"No, I told you that."

"You're not sleeping together? You're not fooling around?"

"No, Cam. Seriously. I'm not dating Leslie or having sex with her or anything."

That's when I emerged from the bathroom.

Matty's face dropped.

"Camilla, can you give me a ride back to my car?" was all I could say.

I was absolutely stunned. Matty looked like he'd been sucker-punched.

I cried in Camilla's passenger seat, and she apologized to me over and over. I was so confused though. I didn't get it.

After that, my life seemed to turn into one nightmarish, drama-filled, codependent Groundhog Day after another. An endless cycle of fighting, breaking up, missing each other, making up, sleeping together, then fighting and breaking up again.

Matty would do his best John Cusack impression and would show up outside of my apartment window with an acoustic guitar singing "The Song" to me when I wouldn't answer his texts or phone calls.

I'd cry, "Didn't you want to marry me on the beach? Didn't you want to have a daughter named Venice with me? Weren't we going to make music together? We were supposed to travel the world and win Grammy awards together! How could you just shit all over our dream like this?"

I was completely disillusioned. There was no way he was going to be able to give me my dream back. But I wanted him to. I wanted him to "fix it" so bad. I wanted him to say something to make it all better. I could care less if he was telling me the truth or lying. If he would just say the right things, we could forget this awful nightmare and go back to our fantasy.

He asked me if I wanted him to quit the band. I said no. Just because he and I weren't going to be a thing, didn't mean we should ruin the band, too. But it was already too late. The other guys in the band had no idea about all the details, but they suspected that something bad was going on between me and Matty. They were not hiding their annoyance.

After a few awkward rehearsals, with Matty showing up almost an hour late and me setting up his drums for him, our lead guitarist had had enough.

"You're fucking using again, Matty, and you're lying about it and it's affecting your performance. You are almost an hour late for rehearsal every week. When I see Leslie setting up your drum kit for you, it just stirs the pot, dude. I am so pissed off at you, man."

I tried to interrupt. Tried to defend Matty. My guitarist cut me off.

"Leslie, no. You don't understand. We go way back. And Matty has a way of doing this shit and ruining everything. We've been through this before. Matty knows what I'm talking about."

He continued, "And by the way, what the fuck is going on with you two?"

The truth was, nothing was going on with us two anymore. Now that I found out he was still sleeping with Camilla.

"Leslie, Matty is a drug addict. He can't handle his drugs. What if we are so lucky to get a record deal and go on tour? How are you going to feel when you find out Matty is hooking up with some groupie?"

I laughed nervously, because I already found out that Matty had lied and cheated on me. And here we were at practice, trying, but failing, to keep *whatever-it-was-that-had-gone-on-with-us* a secret from the other guys in the band.

"You're fucking obsessed with her, Matty. You know, she was like a little sister to us. And no offense, Leslie, but you can be really naïve about things."

He was really fed up. "Nothing is sacred! I thought we told you to stay away from the singer, Matty."

The guys in my band had a secret talk when Matty first joined, and had told Matty to keep his hands off me. This was news to me. Of course, tell someone like Matty not to do something, and he's going to want to do it even more. I was so utterly clueless about addiction back then.

"I'm done with this drama, Matty. I'm quitting this band. I just want to make music and have fun. This is a bunch of bullshit. You're late for rehearsal every night. I could be home hanging out with my wife and my dog." He packed up his guitar and left, followed by our bass player, who only said, "Aww, man. This sucks. I just want to play." And he packed up and left too.

That left just me and Matty in the room, awkwardly looking at each other.

"I can't believe he asked me what I would do if you ever cheated on me. Ohhh, what am I going to do now? The irony," I said sarcastically.

Matty looked down, sighed, and shook his head.

I helped Matty pack up his drums and then he asked me if we could talk. I don't recall the details of what he said, but it was probably whatever I needed to hear. Because we ended up sleeping together. Followed by me having a meltdown because I knew everything was just…so…wrong.

And that was the pattern. I'd want to be with him. But then I didn't trust him. So we'd fight. Then he'd say exactly what I needed to hear. We'd sleep together. Then I'd cry, "I thought you wanted to move into a hip studio downtown with me? Drink wine in a hot air balloon? Have babies in a whirlpool? I don't understand why you lied about Camilla."

Wahh!

Over and over and over again. For two years. During that time, Matty finally admitted everything to me. He had never stopped using. Camilla was using too. She was his supplier.

I thought if only he would quit, it would solve everything. I constantly whined about him. Even my friends were getting annoyed with me. Listening to the same stories about me and Matty and Camilla repeatedly. They would say, "If you're going to give Matty another chance, you need to stop bringing up the past. If you can't forgive him for what happened with Camilla, then you need to move on."

They were right. But I couldn't. I was addicted.

My medical transcription job was outsourced overseas. So I transferred to a different department. My new title was "Management Assistant," but this was just a glorified title for a secretary.

I was a terrible secretary. Terrible at multitasking. My voice was too loud for an office setting. Coworkers were shushing me when I was on the phone with my colleagues. I would screw up the simplest of tasks somehow. All the paperwork looked the same to me. If I was in the middle of doing something and the phone rang, then I would forget what I was initially doing as soon as I got off the phone. So there would always be little projects that would be forgotten and not completed. And office equipment hated me. If I so much as looked at the copy machine it would sputter and break.

Coworkers felt, "Well, you're not stupid, so you must be screwing this up on purpose."

Desk jobs were the bane of my existence. I'd get so overwhelmed I'd zone out and not hear the phone ringing that I was supposed to answer. Overwhelmed, my secretary brain would shut down and my thoughts would go straight to Matty.

When I was at work, I obsessed over what Matty might be doing without me. If he didn't call me when he said he would, I would freak out. If he didn't show up when he said he would, I would freak out.

I'd fight the tears at my desk. My heart was so heavy. I'd run to my car in the parking garage, get in the backseat of my Honda Civic, curl up in the fetal position, and just bawl my eyes out for the entire forty-five-minute lunch break that I had. Then I'd go back to my desk and try unsuccessfully to stop crying.

My manager, John Michael, and the doctors I worked with at Cedars-Sinai were becoming annoyed with me. I was so unprofessional, just losing my shit at my desk all the time. Matty would sometimes try to call me on my work phone, because I wouldn't always answer my flip phone when I saw his name. I remember picking up the phone once, hearing his voice, and then taking the receiver and banging it on my desk, and screaming into the phone, "I wish that was your head" before hanging up on him. When I looked up, one of the doctors I worked with was standing there just looking at me with disgust. Then he just walked away.

I just couldn't take it anymore. I was afraid I was going to lose my job. I wasn't functioning. I was acting crazy. My emotions were spilling out all over the place at the most inappropriate times. So, at the advice of my therapist, I asked my primary care physician to put me on an antidepressant.

Mistake number one. One should never go to a primary care physician for mental health or psychiatric medications without seeing a psychiatrist FIRST. My doctor put me on the antidepressant venlafaxine, which initially helped me get out of my funk. Unfortunately, the medication my doctor chose to give me was absolutely the wrong prescription for my condition.

If you only walk away with one thing, and one thing only, after reading this book, please go to a psychiatrist and not your regular family care provider if you need any psychiatric medications of any kind: antidepressant, anti-psychotic, anti-anxiety, anti-insomniac. If the medication you need has anything to do with your state of mind, go to a psychiatrist! Your regular doctor cares about your well-being and means well, but they really aren't trained the way a psychiatric practitioner is on the subtle nuances of mental health and psychiatric medications. So, other than writing you a refill for something a psychiatrist has already assessed as appropriate for your mental health condition, stick to getting vaccines and antibiotics from your regular doctor and find a psychiatrist for your mental health instead.

The one good piece of advice my therapist had been giving me even before I'd met Matty, was that she felt I could really benefit from going to Adult Children of Alcoholics meetings. That didn't make any sense to me. Neither of my parents even drank alcohol. Maybe a sip of champagne at a wedding, but not much more. I'd feel like an intruder. My therapist tried to explain that the dynamic between a child and mentally ill parent is nearly identical to the dynamic between a child and an alcoholic or addict parent. It all leads to the same type of addictive, codependent behavior and fear of abandonment. With Matty, now that I had a bona fide addict in my life, maybe it was finally time to take my therapist's advice. Thinking I was going to learn the twelve steps to get Matty sober at NarAnon meetings, I was stunned when I was told that I was part of Matty's problem, not his solution. The twelve steps were for ME.

I'd whine in the meetings, "If he really loves me, why won't he stop using meth?"

To which the response was, "You can't quit him, and he can't quit meth. You're the same. You're an addict. You understand him better than you think."

The anxiety and fear that surrounded my feelings for Matty confused me. They were so dark and scary. "If it's hysterical, it's historical," they would say at the meetings. Why was I absolutely hysterical over Matty? Because he triggered old fears and reopened old wounds from my childhood. My body was reacting to old trauma from my mother's mental illness, and from feeling abandoned by my father. If these old traumas didn't exist, Matty would probably never have had this effect on me.

It's one thing to be sad and worried about your loved one using drugs. Being hysterical over it does nothing to help the situation. I would hysterically drive around Los Angeles and Orange County all hours of the night looking for Matty. What outcome was I hoping to gain from this action? Calling him out for being a lying addict? Berating him so I could feel self-righteous? How does this help the present situation in any way at all?

When you're hysterical, you can't think straight. When you're hysterical, you react, you can't respond. If the way you are feeling is so anxious that your fight or flight response has been triggered, it means your body is reacting to old trauma from the past. When you're hysterical, you're not living in the present. Intuition, knowledge, and acceptance of the present is quiet and calm, even when it is disappointing or sad. Anxiety just screams and lies.

Beginning to separate the feelings Matty triggered from my childhood with the help of these meetings and the medication, I slowly started to come out of this dark hole I was in. I never felt as hopeless as I did after my band split up and I lost Matty. They represented the possibility of all my childhood dreams finally coming true. Like Santa Claus, what I was really looking for never existed anyway.

I called Matty's house one night to see where he was. We had plans. He was already over an hour late. His mother was exasperated. She had no idea where he was and admitted he had been acting sketchy again.

"They are going to have to come up with a stronger word than codependent to describe our relationship with Matty," she said. "Me, You, Camilla...we have to stop enabling him. I just don't know how. He's my son."

I understood what she meant. And I decided that night, that if I really gave a shit about what happened to Matty, I had to stop trying to "fix" him. I had to let him go.

I was not going to be his savior. We were not going to ride off into a rock and roll sunset together. He was not going to be forever grateful to me for saving his life. The only person that could save Matty, was Matty. And the only person who could save me, was me.

I kept going to those twelve step meetings until I was able to see myself with clarity. I had been a part of Matty's problem, and I was slowly starting to realize that. My expectations of him had been unrealistic. And I was doing more harm to him than I was helping him. I had become a controlling nag, just as I'd predicted in the song I'd written for him. I literally was treating him the way my fiancé, Trey, had been treating me. As if Matty's journey didn't matter, and I knew what was best for him. The truth was, I had no idea what was good for Matty at all.

I was spiraling downward and still trying to figure out what was good for me.

May 2021

Nowadays, when I think of my cousin Vivian crashing the motorcycle into the woods when she was barely out of kindergarten, I realize my uncle could have acted one of two ways: he could have reacted with fear, or he could have reacted with encouragement.

If he had reacted in fear, he could have punished her, grounded her, and told her to never ride a motorcycle again. He may have instilled in her that the only way to stay safe and not make mistakes and break things, was to not do anything at all. I wonder if he had reacted in fear, if Vivian would be the successful emergency medicine doctor she is today.

That's not what my uncle did, though. Instead, he taught Vivian that if you break something, you don't throw it away. You fix it. You learn how if you don't know. You brush yourself off when you make a mistake, and you try again. If you are afraid, you push through the fear until you're not afraid anymore. After all, you can't learn to be brave if you are never in a vulnerable position. If you've never been broken, how do you learn how to heal?

The author Julie Ann Walker says, "The light only truly shines through people who have been broken."

Matty and I were broken.

I can safely say that twenty years later, we aren't broken anymore.

5

ZEN MOTORCYCLE HABIT #5

IF YOU DON'T KNOW SOMETHING, LEARN

"The place to improve the world is first in one's own heart and head and hands, and then work outward from there."

− Robert Pirsig, Zen and the Art of Motorcycle Maintenance

How I learned things the hard way

Without abusing substances, I didn't realize I was an addict. I was a worse addict than Matty. My addiction to romance was the sweet fix I needed. Without my knowing why, vying for the affection from my latest crush felt better than anything else. This is known as codependency, and I was deep in it.

There is still a lot that the health care community doesn't know about addiction. However, researchers are learning that it has less to do with the substance a person is using, and more to do with that person's brain chemistry, and their body's ability to cope with stress. William R. Lovallo, Ph.D, a research scientist from the V.A. Medical Center, has identified specific genes associated with addiction. There are certain genes involved in regulating the brain's dopamine levels. And

Dr. Lovallo found that if these genes suffer a slight mutation, due to high stress levels in a person's childhood (such as a divorce, or bullying, or sexual abuse), that gene mutation makes a person more susceptible to addiction.

The National Institute on Drug Abuse now recognizes addiction as a brain disease. Some addictions are harder to recognize than others. Codependency and workaholism often fly under the radar, because just about everyone is looking for their soulmate and a decent career.

Another subject I didn't understand was psychiatric pharmaceuticals. This was learned the hard way too!

I didn't understand the difference between antipsychotics, antianxiety medications, or antidepressants. I didn't understand the importance of seeing an actual psychiatrist, and not a regular family practitioner when you need antidepressants or psychiatric medications of any kind. I had seen my mother just get worse and worse the more her doctors tried to medicate her. I wasn't aware of the nuances between them. For a while, I even believed that all psychiatric treatments were bad—that the cure was worse than the disease.

Of course, I had to learn that it was much more complicated than that. Making a correct diagnosis is difficult and finding the right cocktail of medicine to treat a diagnosis is even trickier. If your regular family doctor has put you on the wrong pills, before a psychiatrist has had a chance to see you, they are not going to know where your mental health issue ends, and the drugs begin. I had to learn how difficult it is to make the correct diagnosis. I had to learn that there is more than one way to overcome mental illness.

Summer 2003

Matty and I had been in a codependent circle of hell for the last year or so, and I was not functioning well at all. After my conversation with his mother, I realized I needed to find a way to pull myself together, because I knew my emotional outbursts were not helping Matty, and they were practically destroying me. Up until this time in my life, I'd been afraid to go on any antidepressants or other psychiatric medications after watching my mother deteriorate on them, but my life was unmanageable, and I was getting desperate. After spending all my lunch breaks in the back of my Honda Civic curled up in the fetal position crying over Matty and the loss of my rock and roll dream, I had to do something about it. So, at the advice of my therapist, I went to my primary care doctor's office. When I told her I needed an antidepressant, she asked me why.

"I'm in love with the drummer in my band, and I found out he's addicted to crystal meth," I wailed, then broke into tears.

Validating my sadness, my doctor said, "When a loved one is on drugs, it is almost like grieving a death."

This was when my doctor recommended a specific antidepressant called venlafaxine to me. She confided in me that she recently started taking it herself after her husband died and it helped her get back on her feet.

When I first started taking venlafaxine, I immediately felt amazing. This feeling of absolute euphoria should have been the first red flag.

Soon, I found myself calling up all my friends and relatives.

"I can't believe my mother hated taking her medications so much," I'd tell them, their answering machine, or their voice mail.

"I love being on this medication. Is this how normal people feel? I must have been really sick, because I've never felt this good my whole life!"

Within a few days, I forgot about my problems. Well, I didn't exactly forget about them. I just didn't give a shit about them anymore. My "happy pills" made me feel as though I didn't have to work through anything—the problems that caused me to seek medication in the first place were put on the back burner, simmering. Waiting to explode.

Now, the medication really did help me at first. It pulled me out of a dark hole that I was drowning in. And as a bonus, I didn't feel awkward or anxious in social situations anymore. I did a bunch of positive things that I probably wouldn't have done without it.

For example, I had the energy to go to yoga classes three times a week. I started taking prerequisites for nursing school that I'd been putting off for years. I went on a medical mission to Guatemala with some of my coworkers. Returning to my music, I bought another guitar, found a teacher, and started writing more songs on my own. All this newfound self-confidence was definitely a result of the venlafaxine.

With the help of my new pills, I finally stopped obsessing over Matty. It really threw him off at first. I stopped yelling and screaming at him when he showed up late, or when I caught him in a lie. Catching Matty in a lie and being self-righteous about it had become a fix for me. The medication took the place of my need for a Matty-fix all the time. He actually got mad at me once for not getting mad at him.

"So, are we a couple or not?" he asked me once. He was so used to me freaking out and demanding we label our relationship.

I said, "I'm done trying to label us, Matty. If you're acting like my boyfriend, then you're my boyfriend. If you're not acting like my boyfriend, then you're not my boyfriend. I'm done with words. I want us to act like a couple, not just label us a couple."

It was a good thing for both of us. The venlafaxine was helping me to let go of things I couldn't control. But, after about six months or so, I started to feel like I was over-medicated.

Even though venlafaxine had initially helped me get out of

a depression, it wasn't the right medication for me. It was too strong, and this was apparent when I became manic and impulsive.

If I went to work and missed a dose of venlafaxine, within five hours, my head would be in the garbage can, vomiting. I had become chemically dependent on it. And then I found myself making really impulsive decisions. It was as if venlafaxine had taken the word "No" out of my vocabulary. I said yes to dates with guys I normally wouldn't touch with a ten-foot pole. Yes to going out to dinner when I couldn't afford it. Yes to partying seven days a week and not taking care of my responsibilities. Yes to marrying the Brazilian guy ten years my junior who lives in the apartment downstairs. Yes to telling my boss to fuck off and walking off the job, without another job lined up.

Los Angeles, California, 2004

By the time I was in my mid-thirties, I was no longer enjoying pursuing singing as a career. I liked to sing alone with my guitar in little cafes. I played regularly at the Kibbitz Room behind Canter's Deli on Fairfax, and at O'Brennan's on Lincoln in Venice, but I was done with the idea of becoming a star.

The first season of the show *American Idol* had just started. Friends and fans of previous bands I'd sung in told me I should audition. They said I had the type of voice for that show. But I was feeling disillusioned after my last band broke up. I didn't want to continue on that journey anymore.

At the same time, I was freaking out because I didn't know what I was supposed to do with myself anymore. Without that singular focus in my life, I felt like I was a lonely wet T-shirt just blowing in the breeze.

Matty was inconsistent and I wasn't relying on him anymore. Venlafaxine had helped me to loosen the grip I had been holding onto. Once I'd found interests of my own and a new group of friends, Matty stopped being the center of my universe. If Matty didn't call me when I was expecting to hear from him, I'd just turn off my phone and fall asleep at night. Whatever it was Matty was doing or not doing, I was no longer taking his behavior personally. I finally got it, that nothing he was doing was a reflection of me. After he had disappeared for several months, I started dating someone else exclusively.

Tiago moved into my apartment building after Matty had gone missing again. He was from Brazil and could barely speak English. After we'd dated for about two months, and I'd been on venlafaxine for about two years, Tiago asked me to marry him one night while we were watching Netflix. He made it clear it was for a green card.

"Sure. Why not?!"

Since I wasn't going to be a rock star after all (nor did I want to be), I had nothing better to do. Getting married to the first person who asked didn't seem like such a bad idea at the time.

Not only did I agree, but I decided to do an astrological experiment. Tiago and I got married at 3:30 a.m. on a Tuesday. There was a new moon in Libra, the sign of marriage and contracts. I thought maybe, just maybe, it would turn into a real marriage. Being that it was so close to Halloween, and since we decided to get married in the middle of the night, Tiago wanted to have a Halloween-themed wedding. We lived down the street from one of Los Angeles's most popular costume stores, Robinson's Beautilities. Tiago decided we should rent their Cleopatra and Mark Anthony costumes. I must admit, Tiago kind of looked adorable, like Marvin the Martian from Looney Tunes with that Mark Anthony head-piece on. I could have sworn I saw Carol and Mike from *The Brady Bunch* in these same exact same outfits during a Halloween episode. The woman who married us was dressed up like a Greek goddess with a crown of leaves and we encouraged all my friends to get dressed up in costumes as well. Tiago was friends with a guy who owned a hip-hop clothing store less than a block from our apartment called "Buckwyld" and we could exchange our nuptials there after hours. A friend of mine who was going to culinary school catered our grand celebration with little pastry puffs full of gourmet cheeses with obnoxious French names, and some California-Mexican-Asian fusion hors d'oeuvres.

Of course, my friends were like, "You're getting married at 3:30 a.m. to that guy who's ten years younger than you, who you've only been dating for two months? Oh...kay... We'll be there."

They all put on happy, supportive faces for me, but were quietly whispering to each other through fake smiles and gritted teeth, "What the fuuuuck is she doing? This shit is craaaazy."

I didn't realize that the medication was clouding my judgement. I already had a hard enough time making adult decisions for myself. Venlafaxine was putting me over the edge. It was not allowing me to deal with the root of my depression. It was hard to see how irrational I was behaving. Not on illegal drugs, but still high as a kite from antidepressants.

I had to learn that, too.

What is perfectly clear now, is that I had been prescribed the wrong class of antidepressant by my primary care provider. Not all antidepressants are created equally. A medication that stops one person from hanging themselves, may cause a different person to become manic. My therapist really should have advised me to see an actual psychiatrist with expertise in psychotropic medications. Over the years, I have been misdiagnosed with ADHD, bipolar disorder, borderline personality disorder, and generalized anxiety disorder. That's because no psychiatrist ever saw me at baseline.

They only saw me high on venlafaxine.

After a while, all the things I wasn't dealing with while on venlafaxine started to creep back up on me. I was paranoid and felt like shit. In addition to the medication making me balloon out like Stevie Nicks on klonopin, all the eating out and drinking I couldn't afford helped me to pack on an additional thirty pounds. At just over five feet tall, thirty pounds made me about 30 percent larger than my frame was used to carrying. I felt out of breath from carrying the extra weight.

Meanwhile, back at work in my glorified secretary position, I was screwing up the simplest of tasks constantly, and my managers were pissed off. Sometimes, they'd just send me home from work. "I can't pay you to just sit here and surf the internet," one of them once said.

With no litmus test for normal, I didn't realize how much I was spinning out of control.

February 2021

One morning not long after I bought my motorcycle, I totally forgot that I was cooking a hard-boiled egg. Much in the way that my emotions had simmered under the mask of venlafaxine, I just left the egg on the stove until the boiling water evaporated and it exploded. Hearing a loud pop while I was taking a shower, I emerged from the bathroom to find my kitchen was smoky and smelled like a burnt fart. As I began picking pieces of the exploded egg off the walls and ceiling, I thought to myself, "I have no business riding a motorcycle."

When it came to learning about motorcycles, I had sold myself short in the past. I would tell myself things like, "I'm too irresponsible to ride a motorcycle, as evidenced by my almost burning down my apartment complex while cooking an egg."

I'm too short, too small, and not strong enough. I'm too much of a wuss, I'm too fearful, and I'll be too anxious to focus. I'll make a stupid mistake and get myself killed. I'm too clumsy and I'll drop it. I'm too afraid and I don't know how to overcome my fear.

Honestly, I believed that I had no business trying to learn to ride a motorcycle. I was certain that the universe would punish me for even trying. I'd be punished for having the audacity to do something so reckless and dangerous. Every mistake I made when I was learning to ride, I took as a sign that I shouldn't be riding.

I spent nearly eight months in a boring parking lot. It was hard for me to remain patient with myself. Would it have been easier if I bought a different motorcycle? A cheaper one at that? Or maybe I needed to buy a scooter to practice on? Would that be less intimidating? I think my bike has too much torque. It's too powerful for me. Maybe I should sell it.

But I persisted.

I kept fighting my old urges to give up and label motorcycles as one more thing that was "not meant for me." Plus, I spent a pretty penny on this electric motorcycle, and I had to make it worth the purchase.

I wasn't going to give up. If it was going to take me over a year to learn to ride this thing, I was going to do it. Many times, in the parking lot, I thought about giving up. I had a hard time just enjoying the process. So I was just going to have to keep on learning the skills necessary to ride, until my fear subsided, and I finally learned to trust myself.

When I was with Matty, it wasn't easy for me to admit that there were things I needed to learn. It was easy for me to just blame him for everything. I wanted things to be black or white. In other words, someone had to be wrong, and someone had to be right. Blaming the "drug addict" for everything was easy.

The truth is, there were two people involved in that relationship. I had contributed my own toxic baggage to the situation and when I realized this, I beat myself up. A lot.

However, if we want to, we can make it really easy on

ourselves. There is no need to mentally flog yourself just because you didn't know something. We are capable of learning and changing our direction. New information doesn't have to disrupt your world. If you want to, you can simply say: "*I didn't know that before. But now that I know, I want to do better.*"

When we stop learning, we stop living. Keep your mind open to the truth. When you are learning anything in life, expect setbacks. Setbacks are not a sign that you should give up. A person who has never failed, has never tried.

June 2021

Today, I am not only a psychiatric nurse, but also a chemical dependency nurse. In the past, I have worked in the full gamut of psychiatric and mental health settings. From suburban New Jersey to Skid Row to Malibu. From psychiatric crisis stabilization urgent care to long-term inpatient units. From detox centers to adolescent psychiatric units.

Once upon a time, I was completely clueless and naïve about addiction. I thought I was in control and could fix other people. I didn't understand why you don't go to a primary care physician for psychotropic drugs, either. Today, addiction and mental health nursing are my expertise. I didn't understand before, but I learned.

6

ZEN MOTORCYCLE HABIT #6

IF YOU FALL DOWN, GET BACK UP

"If you have made mistakes, there is always another chance for you. You can start over any moment you choose...It's not the falling down that counts. It's the getting up."

—MARY PICKFORD

How I learned to pick myself back up after falling

The night before I checked myself into the psych ward, I was at a rave up in Simi Valley. I have no idea where Tiago, my green card husband, was that evening. But I'm sure he had left the house in a huff. My behavior continued to freak him out, and a language barrier just made it worse. It took a few months for me to realize, he really didn't understand English as well as he could speak it. Certain jokes and sarcasm did not translate well from English to Brazilian Portuguese. So I'd gone out to meet up with some friends without him.

At the Simi Valley Rave up on some ranch on a hill, a friend handed me a neon-blue alcoholic beverage. I chugged it, then tripped and fell down in the dirt, vomiting all over myself. This was not my finest moment. My state of mind was even more frayed than it had been a year ago.

I wanted to get off venlafaxine. This was easier said than done. I was flying higher than Icarus and my wings were about to burn. It made me forget everything that was upsetting me. It had been about three years since I began therapy, and I still wasn't addressing the root of my problems. The medication was not actually letting me deal with reality. All the things I wasn't dealing with while taking these meds finally caught up with me. I became a disorganized mess—flying high and manic from an antidepressant.

I started seeing a psychiatrist, but he only knew me when I was high on venlafaxine. This led to a misdiagnosis of bipolar disorder. When the medications that are usually prescribed for bipolar disorder didn't work for me, I was misdiagnosed with borderline personality disorder (BPD). My friends were more insulted by that diagnosis than I was. I also hate taking physical risks, which is a key feature of those with borderline personality disorder. In fact, those with BPD often don't live very long because of the risks they take.

Yes, I know. I ride a motorcycle. But you have to understand, learning to ride a motorcycle was so outside of the box for me. Literally, I created ten new life habits in order to even BEGIN to start learning to ride. I spent nearly eight months riding around in a parking lot because I was absolutely terrified of my motorcycle. I even wondered if I'd made a huge mistake the first two to three months I owned it. My surfing career was aborted for similar reasons: because I was having panic attacks. To avoid living on my own in the big scary world, I lived with my dad until I was almost twenty-nine. To put it mildly, it is not in my regular nature to gamble or take big risks.

As a result of my misdiagnoses, I spent the next fifteen years struggling emotionally, feeling ashamed, and getting drugged up on the wrong medications.

The night of the Simi Valley rave and the now infamous blue cocktail from hell was the culmination of many disappointing and distressing life events, only made worse by venlafaxine.

I felt like the best parts of my life were over—it was all downhill from here now. Without music to pursue, I wasn't anyone special anymore. An L.A. washout, just another nobody. I had no idea what to do with myself, if my career as a singer was done. What else did I have to offer?

To add insult to injury, my medical transcription job at Cedars-Sinai had been outsourced overseas. Unable to find a position as a transcriber, the only thing I was qualified to do was attempt to become a secretary. Yet I was absolutely the worst secretary and receptionist ever.

Before my hospitalization, I'd been trying to complete prerequisites for nursing school. However, chemistry class was kicking my ass. I dropped the class when I couldn't get approved for a student loan. What was the point? It was a waste.

July 2005

Anyhow, the morning after the disastrous Simi Valley rave, I called up my psychiatrist and said that my brain didn't feel right. He told me to have a friend drop me off at the UCLA emergency room. I remember my first day in the psych unit was the Fourth of July. On theme, they had a BBQ with hot dogs and hamburgers in the psychiatric unit's courtyard. I hoped it was an auspicious sign; this would be my Independence Day from depression and suicidal ideations.

I spent two weeks in the psychiatric unit. At the hospital, I stayed on venlafaxine. My health care providers tried adding other medications to my routine: Cymbalta, Geodon, Lexapro, Strattera, and Lithium, among others.

The psychiatrists and nurses in the psychiatric unit at

UCLA were extremely compassionate and good at their jobs. Before my hospitalization, I had been trying to get into nursing school. Now, I was worried that the stigma of being hospitalized for a psychiatric disorder would prevent me from becoming a nurse. Yet my health care providers at UCLA were all very encouraging. They told me about Kay Redfield, a famous psychiatrist who suffers from bipolar disorder herself. She had spent time on UCLA's psychiatric unit, and had written a number of books that are now considered the gold standard textbooks on bipolar disorder today. She is said to have revolutionized psychiatric treatment. Maybe there was hope for me, too.

Instead, I got addicted to food, as well as addicted to cigarettes, while I was there. We were served meals that were prepared by the UCLA culinary students. I remember one particularly delicious dish: halibut in garlic butter and asparagus. The staff on the psychiatric unit kept all the patients stocked with cigarettes. Even though I hadn't been a tobacco smoker before, I figured, what the fuck, might as well smoke, too.

I was discharged after two weeks on lithium and still on venlafaxine. I felt relieved that Lithium was working for me because it wasn't a controlled substance and had no reputation for being addictive. All I wanted was to be normal and fit into society, not looked down on as a crazy person.

My joy was short-lived.

Within three months of being prescribed lithium, my small, 5'1" frame had packed on an extra forty pounds and my face looked swollen, broken out like a pizza. My hair and nails became brittle, and I felt extremely insecure and ugly. My friends were astonished. They thought my acne must have been induced by meth use, even though I'd never done meth in my life. Plus, I was still acting a little erratic. Even on the lithium.

The lithium helped my state of mind, but it wreaked

havoc on my body. Even when I was eating salads and drinking water with lemon, the pounds kept piling on. I joined a gym. I spent a mere twenty minutes on the elliptical. The next day I could barely move. I had put my back out because it wasn't strong enough to carry the weight I'd packed onto my little body. Both my body and my mind felt weak. My moods would swing a dozen times on any given day.

I was still making impulsive decisions. Like when I was rebounding from Matty and married Tiago after dating two months. I rationalized that I didn't want my new boyfriend to have to leave the country, so I married him. But it had been an impulsive thing to do.

August 2005

It had now been at least a year since Matty disappeared. I had just finished spending two weeks in UCLA's psychiatric facility, when one day, I got an unexpected phone call from him. He was apologizing for having gone missing. He had finally used up his last get-out-of-jail-for-free card. Third strike in California. He told me he went to prison for six months. For meth. But he was sober now. Without help from me, Camilla, or his mother, Matty was finally sober. Going to prison saved his life. Matty was speaking with clarity, he wasn't lying to me. He was trying to make amends.

I was still a long way off from saving myself, though. Matty's recovery was going along a lot faster than mine. Once again, I felt like I couldn't keep up. It was ironic that I was now the one who wasn't sober. No, I wasn't taking illegal drugs, but I wasn't sober. My drugs were legal from the pharmacy and taken as prescribed, but I had become chemically dependent on venlafaxine. Not having addressed any of the reasons I needed it in the first place, I was impaired.

I hadn't done anything to help get Matty sober. He went to prison. And that's how Matty got sober.

Without me, his mother, or Camilla enabling him anymore, Matty got sober. He fixed himself. Just like I had to fix myself.

"I saw you got married when I was on social media...I cried when I saw that," Matty said. He was trying to make it sound like he had cried tears of joy. But I could hear it in his voice, he was sad. Matty's voice was cracking, because he was worried about me. I wasn't making any sense.

I was so fucked up on psychiatric medications, I barely remember the whole conversation. Matty was trying to tell me how he had finally gotten sober. How he'd gotten back involved in his church. How he was trying to heal his life. It was all great news. He had really struggled. He had faced his demons. He was a minister now.

Jaded, I was thinking, "Oh, fuck this self-righteous asshole and his fucking religion."

Matty said, "Les, it's me. I'm not some born-again Jesus freak. Well, okay, maybe I am. But, it's still me, Les. I'm the person you always thought I was."

"Oh, give me a break," I said. "You think you're safe in your church? None of us are safe. It's all bullshit. You're not safe there either, you know."

"Les. What are you talking about?" Matty was perplexed.

"You know what I'm talking about.'"

I didn't even know what I was talking about.

The last thing I remember him saying was, "I'll pray for you."

Why the fuck would I need his prayers? How insulting. I was fine, although being raised by a loving and sweet, but schizophrenic, mother, made it difficult to envision what "fine" was. I was definitely not "fine." Freaking out more and more every day, I dreaded morphing into my severely mentally ill mother. Unfortunately, it took a medical bankruptcy and painful withdrawal from venlafaxine to heal.

I still had so much more to learn. And the road was long and difficult.

That was the last time I ever spoke to Matty.

I saw him on social media, though. He's no longer in California. He's happily married with four kids. He's still a minister. Like, Baptizing people and shit. He looks so happy and healthy. When I saw all this on Instagram, my heart just soared.

But I hope if he reads this, he recognizes himself. I want him to know that my love for him was real, but I just didn't know what real love was then. So many of the things I did and said to him, I thought I had been saying out of love. I now realize they were really said out of fear and a need to control. I take my responsibility for my part in creating more pain and resentment than necessary. I want to tell him his mother was right about everything. I want him to know how proud of him I am.

And I want him to know I will always love him for forcing me to save my own life.

December 2005

The venlafaxine I'd been on for a year and a half, which had initially freed me from the darkest corners of my mind, was really beginning to debilitate me. When Tiago had first met me, I'd been taking venlafaxine for under a year. But after about a year of being in a relationship with me, Tiago grew confused by my behavior as the venlafaxine continued to cloud my judgement. As the things I wasn't dealing with started to back up on me, he thought I must be cheating on him. I wasn't. Based on my greasy skin and cystic acne, no one was breaking down my door to fuck me.

Tiago packed up his stuff one night a few weeks before Christmas and left me. We had broken up after we got into a fight when I was talking on the phone with one of my friends.

I was recalling a night when I accidentally walked into a metal pole.

"Oh my god. I gave myself a black eye! I was like, 'Ahhh! What happened??!'" I said on the phone recalling the event.

Suddenly, Tiago freaked out and scolded me, "I can't believe you are talking about this right in front of me."

"Wait, what are you upset about?" I asked him.

"You know exactly why I'm upset."

The next day when I was at work, Tiago sent me an email saying he was sorry he freaked out on me. He said, "I just couldn't stand thinking about you with that black dude."

"What black dude?"

"Just forget about it."

It took me a couple weeks to realize why Tiago had freaked out.

When I said, "I gave myself a black eye when I walked into a pole! Ahhh!" All Tiago heard was, "Gave myself...black guy...pole...Ahhh!"

He thought I had been talking about having sex with some black guy when I was on the phone. WTF? When I confronted Tiago with my discovery, I could see him trying to stifle a laugh (and if we hadn't gotten into such a bad fight over it, it really would have been hysterical).

A few weeks after Tiago moved out in December, we got together one night and agreed the marriage wasn't going to work. We were going to stay friends, but also stay married, because we only needed to be married for ten more months and then he could get his green card.

Spring 2006

Continuing to spiral downward, every now and then Tiago would bring me groceries because I was still having trouble just taking care of my basic needs. He wouldn't stay long, though. It was too painful and confusing for him to watch the dumpster fire that I'd become. He was just trying to help me keep my shit together until he could get that green card.

My Uncle Cesar, who is my godfather, started sending me checks for $300 a month to help me, after my cousin Mary Ellen had become worried after a phone call with me.

I was scaring my friends. They didn't understand why my behavior was so erratic. A lot of friends just stopped calling me back. Some friends had the decency to tell me they needed a "break" from our friendship because I was acting so weird. It was freaking everyone out. I was ashamed and wanted to disappear.

After one particularly dark weekend, I called up my friend Andy and made him promise he'd take care of my pit bull Phoebe if anything happened to me. Disturbing images of my body in the bathtub bleeding out from slashed wrists plagued my thoughts.

The venlafaxine that I was taking as prescribed seemed to be making me even more miserable and confused than I already was. I'd had enough and was ready to check out of this shitty motel known as planet earth.

While I was eyeing a razor blade and fantasizing about sharp cuts to my wrists, my pit bull, Phoebe, wandered into the bathroom and started kissing my face. My good orange and white girl's big pink tongue snapped me back into reality. I couldn't stand the thought of my dog looking at my dead body in the tub, just bleeding out while my eyes stared lifeless at the ceiling. It was time to try another psych ward. This was my second hospitalization, and I was starting to see a pattern. The more I was listening to my doctors, the worse I was getting. Not only that, my first hospitalization had left me bankrupt when my insurance company decided they didn't want to cover it.

I regretted the day I listened to my therapist and went to my primary care provider to get an antidepressant like a good patient. Now, because it was not the right one, my life was spiraling downward. None of my psychiatrists had ever seen me off venlafaxine, so I was being misdiagnosed and over-medicated constantly.

So now, I found myself hospitalized a second time. I was somewhere in Torrance, I think. This was not UCLA. There were no halibut dinners with garlic butter and asparagus Hollandaise here. If you weren't suicidal when you arrived, you would be after eating the macaroni and cheese laced with cut-up hotdogs they served for dinner. A young woman who looked like she'd been wearing the same mini dress for the past thirty-six hours was escorted onto the unit by two young police officers. She was laughing maniacally and acting completely psychotic.

Sitting on a bench with her hands cuffed behind her back, she screamed, "I'm going to bite your cocks off, as soon as I am done assassinating Saddam Hussein."

The police officers tried their best to remain professional, but the cock comment had them chuckling. Encouraged by their laughter, she kept going, "Yeah, it's all fun and games until you suck MY cock!" The nurse called the two officers over to sign some paperwork. The young woman who was handcuffed to the bench looked over at me. Suddenly, her demeanor completely changed.

"Sweetie," she said in a soothing voice to me, "why are you crying? You don't belong here. Everything is going to be all right. I promise."

"Thank you."

Two minutes later when the officers came back to get her, she went right back to her previous rant. She kept saying the most outrageous shit just to get these two cops to laugh.

"Do you guys, like, hide your guns in your butts? You should try hiding your guns in your butts! I bet you cops play all kinds of Butthole Olympics down at the station!" Was the last thing I heard her say as they led her off to who-knows-where?

After enjoying my gourmet psych ward cuisine of Velveeta macaroni and hotdogs, I decided I'd had enough. I took the butter knife that had come with my meal and brought it into the restroom with me thinking I could cut my wrists with it. My fears had come to pass. I was my mother after all. After focusing so hard on not ending up like her, that was my inevitable path. And here I was. Sitting on the dirty floor. Sawing at my wrists with a butter knife. Suicidal.

Then I had a eureka moment.

Nobody was going to help me. I was just going to have to figure it out for myself. I didn't need anyone to save me. I was going to have to save myself. There was no genius shrink who would make me feel normal, or a mind-blowing fairytale romance to fix my life. There wasn't any combination of pills that was going to solve my problems. It didn't matter what my diagnosis was, I was going to do everything I needed to do to pick myself back up.

So I said all the right things to get myself discharged from the hospital. "No, I'm not suicidal. No, I'm not homicidal. I just had a bad night. I'll go make another appointment with my psychiatrist after I'm discharged."

Suicide was not an option anymore. After all, I was not a murderer.

I decided I was going to get off venlafaxine on my own, no matter what. None of my doctors were listening to me. They didn't believe me when I'd try to tell them what I was experiencing. They didn't believe me when I told them I'd never been manic before and my manic episodes were too short to fit the diagnosis of bipolar. I knew that venlafaxine was the problem. My body had become chemically dependent on it.

In 2006, the economy was tanking in Los Angeles. It was getting difficult to find a job. My trade, medical transcription, had been outsourced overseas. There were more licensed cannabis dispensaries in town than there were Starbucks. So, unable to find any other job that would pay at least $18/hour,

I took a part-time job at a dispensary. I was hoping to save up enough money to go to nursing school. By the time I started working at Sympathetic Tea, a legal medical cannabis dispensary in West Hollywood, I had managed to get off all my psychiatric meds except for venlafaxine.

One day, I was taking a break on the outdoor patio with some of my coworkers. They were all discussing what medications they no longer needed to take because of medical cannabis. They turned to me and started asking me about what medications I was taking.

Unbeknownst to me, some of my colleagues had noticed my behavior was off and were concerned I was on the wrong medications. They felt my upbeat demeanor was a bit too "artificial."

They were 100 percent correct. These young dispensary workers had noticed something my psychiatrists at the time had missed. Many of my coworkers has been in similar situations to mine. So they knew exactly what it looked like when someone was on the wrong medication.

"Do you WANT to be on that med? Do you think you really need it?" my dispensary coworker, Phill, asked me.

"No, I don't. I hate the way venlafaxine makes me feel. I feel like I'm walking around on Ecstasy all day long. I know it's clouding my judgement. I know I'm coming off awkward and hyper. I've tried to stop taking it, but I can't."

What I ended up learning the hard way, was that venlafaxine has a half-life of about five hours. When a drug has a short half-life, it means the medication leaves your body quickly. When a drug leaves your body quickly, your body starts looking for it and becomes chemically dependent on it. I learned this a little too late.

If I didn't take my venlafaxine in the morning at the same exact time every day, withdrawal symptoms would begin within five hours of my missed dose. These symptoms are like withdrawal from many other substances: headache, nausea, and subsequent vomiting. The vomiting was out of control, though and it would happen without warning. It didn't matter where I was when this happened. The shopping mall, the beach, the cafeteria at work. My body didn't care. If I'd forgotten to take my medication that morning, I'd be vomiting like Linda Blair in *The Exorcist* within five hours.

Unfortunately, my primary care provider, not being a psychiatrist (or not having read the warning label) didn't know this when she prescribed it to me.

"The problem is the withdrawal symptoms," I explained. "I stopped all my meds except one. It makes me feel so nauseous and crazy when I don't take it, I'm afraid it will make it hard for me to work. I don't want to be having withdrawals and throwing up in front of customers. I can't afford to take off work. But I don't know how to get off this medication without it interrupting the rest of my life, or my job."

"Sweetheart, tell JoAnna," Phill advised me.

JoAnna was the clinical director of Sympathetic Tea, a kind of godmother of legal weed. She was a licensed pharmacist for over twenty years. She specialized in plant-based medicines after working as a CVS pharmacist and a hospice pharmacist. Once, she lived on a commune and grew tomatoes for Whole Foods Market. She was such an icon, educated but earthy. I looked up to her.

So I knocked on JoAnna's office door and told her, "The guys think I should try to get off the last of my psychiatric medications and see how I feel. But the withdrawals are really bad. They said I should let you know."

"Oh, my goodness, I think that's wonderful," JoAnna said. "That's totally fine, I support you in this. If you need breaks or time off, you just let me know."

Basically, I went through withdrawals from venlafaxine while I worked at the dispensary. If I got dizzy, they'd let me sit in the back and someone else would take over a sale for me. So nauseous at times I could barely eat, I was throwing everything up. They baked me a lasagna that had been cooked in cannabis-infused olive oil, and that was one of the first things I was able to keep down.

The negative aspects of cannabis have been discussed ad nauseam. There are people who do have problems with abusing cannabis. However, while using cannabis as a medicine is controversial, opinions are changing fast. According to the father of toxicology and physician, Paracelsus, "the only real difference between medicine and poison is the dose…and intent." Putting aside my preconceived notions about potheads and cannabis, I did what I needed to do find peace of mind…and keep my dinner down.

It wasn't just one thing or one person who helped me get back up. I had to do whatever I could. Friends, colleagues, and doctors I'd met through Sympathetic Tea, seeing my suffering, offered me free treatments of acupuncture and reiki. One of my patients gave me a gift certificate for a massage. I was not used to going outside of the medical establishment for my healthcare. However, I welcomed the help. I stayed open-minded, humble, and grateful, and accepted their ideas. In return, they gave me my life back.

It doesn't matter how many times you fall in life. What matters is that you keep getting back up. Every time you fall, it is just another opportunity to learn how to rise up again.

January 2021

It's fifteen years later and I am now a nurse myself. I find myself in the middle of the Covid-19 pandemic, traveling from one emergency room to another all over Los Angeles, putting people on involuntary seventy-two-hour psychiatric holds, known as a 5150 Hold, when a patient is a danger to themselves, others, or catatonic from psychosis. There's been a spike in suicidal and homicidal ideations in the population.

The stress of the pandemic is literally driving people crazy. Everyone's anxiety levels are at an all-time high.

One afternoon, a coworker hands me a toasted white-chocolate mocha from Starbucks and I can't taste it. The only thing we know of that causes a loss of taste is Covid. I am immediately sent home to quarantine for at least ten days. Luckily, I don't have any other symptoms. However, as I'm sitting home on my couch, watching the United States Capitol fall into chaos on television, I realize I have been in a constant state of panic for the past couple of years. Now I am slowing down long enough to realize I haven't been managing my depression, stress, or anxiety very well at all. Because of my awful experience on venlafaxine, I haven't been on an antidepressant or any psychiatric medications for about fifteen years at this point but realize I'm needing help. Luckily, I'm wiser now than I was fifteen years ago. As a psychiatric nurse, I have now come to understand the importance of going to a psychiatrist when in need of psychiatric medications and guidance about their use.

During one particularly bad meltdown during this time, I texted a friend of mine who is a psychiatric nurse practitioner. He thought maybe I needed to be on a drug called Lamictal, a mood stabilizer. So he referred me to one of his colleagues. Around this same time, I had an appointment with my primary care doctor and mentioned to him that I planned to see a new psychiatrist. He had his prescription pad out and was ready to prescribe lamictal to me. However, this time, I told him I'd wait until I saw my new psychiatrist. I'd already made the mistake of letting a non-psychiatrist prescribe psychotropic drugs to me in the past with terrible results. I learned not to make that same mistake twice.

It wasn't easy to go back to a psychiatrist after what I'd been through with venlafaxine. Particularly after most of my doctors at that time were not aware that there are people whose lives have nearly been ruined by venlafaxine.

Constantly feeling like my previous psychiatrists were not hearing my truth when I shared my history with them, I'd grown jaded. Most medical doctors and even most psychiatrists are not aware that venlafaxine only has a five-hour half-life, which leads to chemical dependency. They are not aware that the database of Netherlands Pharmacovigilance Centre has collected data showing that there is evidence that hypomania, sexual disinhibition, and spontaneous erections have been associated with the use of venlafaxine.

When I told my *new* psychiatrist that I'd been diagnosed with bipolar disorder, he was not convinced. He was the first psychiatrist to ever assess me off venlafaxine. He was the first psychiatrist I ever worked with who had seen the downside of venlafaxine with some of his other patients, too. He believed it was because I'd been prescribed the wrong medication that I had been misdiagnosed as bipolar. I had never behaved in a manic way off venlafaxine. I had no history of manic behavior previously. My new psychiatrist believed that I was, indeed, on the spectrum, and was not suffering from a psychiatric disorder after all. He put me on sertraline for depression. These drugs did not make me high. They didn't make me forget my problems. Instead, they helped me deal with my struggles. An even bigger blessing is that my new psychiatrist has had years of experience dealing with patients whose lives had nearly been ruined by venlafaxine. "I can only imagine how crazy and awful it must have been for you," he told me during my first visit with him. I finally felt like a validated human being.

On sertraline, getting out of bed and taking a shower no longer seemed like an insurmountable task. Showing up on time for appointments no longer felt like climbing Mount Everest. I didn't have the urge to call up all my friends and family and tell them how great I felt. I could still feel sadness. I could still cry when it was appropriate. And finally, I could now begin to deal with the things that had made me depressed in the first place.

That's because I did not have bipolar disorder, ADHD, or borderline personality disorder. I found out after my fifty-first birthday that I was on the spectrum. As it turns out, the number one misdiagnosis for women who are on the spectrum is borderline personality disorder. The reason I had not had any positive results with the medications or treatments I was under, was because I was being treated for the wrong diagnosis.

And it wasn't easy to get the correct diagnoses either. I had to advocate for myself. I had to do my own research. I had to keep going to different doctors until I found the correct diagnosis and treatment. I had to keep believing in myself even though I felt like I was an imposter. Even when I felt insecure about myself.

Lesson learned. I took one for the team, so you don't have to. I'm repeating this because it's so important: If you need any psychiatric medications at all: antidepressant, anti-anxiety, anti-insomnia, anti-psychotic, etc., do not get them from your regular primary care provider. Get a referral to a psychiatrist so you don't end up on a merry-go-round of misdiagnoses like I did.

Bryan Kest, one of my favorite yoga teachers while I was living in Los Angeles, used to say how much he loves it when his students fall down and lose their pose. It gives them the opportunity to learn how to get back up again.

And what is really more important in life than learning how to get back up again?

June 2021

For some reason, dropping a motorcycle feels so devastating. Even if you don't get hurt. And even if the bike is barely scratched. There is something about dropping a motorcycle that makes you feel like you can't trust yourself. A mixture of fear, embarrassment, and dread comes over you. You consciously think, "Okay. Big deal. I dropped my motorcycle. I'm not hurt. It's not hurt. Why can't I just be Zen about it?"

The anxiety of learning to ride a motorcycle for me was so bad at times, I'd find myself having a full-on panic attack just watching YouTube videos of my favorite motovloggers. One time I found myself having an anxiety attack just looking at pictures of motorcycles on the internet, and thought to myself, "How in the hell am I ever going to be able to learn to ride safely if I break into a panic just looking at a motorcycle?"

I have dropped every single motorcycle that I have ever ridden. I started on a Yamaha V-Star 250 at the Motorcycle Safety Foundation course in Long Beach. I loved the look of it, such a cute little cruiser. After riding around on it for a few hours, I found myself getting mentally fatigued. I hit the throttle when I was trying to pull in the brake and ended up on the ground.

The instructor asked me if I was interested in taking the course on a bike with an automatic transmission. She suggested I take a private lesson to learn to shift gears later. She was trying to help keep me from getting overwhelmed. And I was so grateful she gave me that option, even though I kind of felt like I was chickening out of the challenge. Also, I didn't want to hold up the rest of the class. I've always hated that I have a hard time keeping up with others. The bike with the automatic transmission was a 2011 Zero XU electric motorcycle. I fell in love with it. And about a half an hour after getting on it, I dropped that bike too.

Luckily, I didn't drop any more motorcycles during the course. Three drops and you get kicked out and have to come back and retake the entire course. Somehow, I was able to pass the course and get my motorcycle license.

The first bike I bought was a KX85 dirt-bike. My husband felt very strongly that I needed to ride a dirt-bike. He felt it was safer for me to make all mistakes in the dirt far away from traffic. But going dirt-bike riding, even if just for an hour or two, was a major undertaking. And I was desperate to start practicing on a bike, any bike.

To go dirt-bike riding, we had to pack up the truck. Then we had to tow the bikes on a trailer, after getting them all gassed up. After that, we'd have to drive nearly two hours away to get to the trails. So I really needed a street bike I could practice on.

Based on my experience with the 2011 Zero XU, I bought myself a 2021 Zero S Electric Motorcycle. I didn't even test ride it. I knew it was more powerful than the XU, but I figured I grow into it.

The first day I took my bike out, I underestimated a U-Turn I was trying to make and ended up going onto the sidewalk. Then I hit the throttle without realizing it and ended up slamming myself into the ground. I ordered some drop bars to protect the bike. I put them on, and then tried again.

The second time I took my bike out, I did the same thing. I was coming to the end of a parking-lot practice session and pulled into a parking space. I felt a little unsteady when I was stopping. To stop the bike from tipping over, I instinctively grabbed the "handlebar," which is actually the throttle. I nearly sent the bike into the stratosphere. A split second later I was on the ground, facing 180 degrees in the opposite direction, tires smoking behind me.

The third time I took my bike out, I didn't even ride it. I put a rug down in the driveway and I had my husband lay the bike down on its side for me. Then I practiced picking up all 350 pounds of it by myself. I thought if I knew how to pick up a dropped motorcycle by myself, then I wouldn't be afraid to drop it.

The fourth time I took my bike out, I did the same damn thing. I hit the throttle by accident when I was trying to stop.

But this time, I was able to pick up the motorcycle all by myself.

The fifth time I took my motorcycle out, I didn't drop it. Nor did I drop it the time after that, or the time after that. I haven't dropped a motorcycle since. If I had given up the first or second time I dropped the bike, I wouldn't be riding. Even when I'm unsteady during a stop, I feel in control of my bike and can correct it without ending up on the ground. But that is because I picked myself up every single time after I fell.

What matters in life is that you get back up every time, no matter how hard it is or however long it takes. It is no different on the bike than it is in life.

It took me a long time to learn to trust myself after falling. To not relive my past mistakes and to ground myself in the present. It's something I have to constantly re-evaluate, practice, and put in check, in order to stay in this place.

I had to fall down a lot, both on the motorcycle and in life, to learn how to pick myself up again.

And I wasn't done falling down just yet.

7

ZEN MOTORCYCLE HABIT #7

LOOK IN THE DIRECTION YOU WANT TO GO, NOT WHERE YOU DON'T WANT TO GO

"You look at where you're going and where you are and it never makes sense, but then you look back at where you've been, and a pattern seems to emerge."

—ROBERT M. PIRSIG, ZEN AND THE ART OF MOTORCYCLE MAINTENANCE

How I almost ended up just like my mother when I was trying not to end up just like my mother

I had a therapist in college. She told me, "If there are two alcoholics, and only two alcoholics, watching a sold-out football game at Giants Stadium, they will manage to find one another and get drunk together."

"Like attracts like," she said, "and whatever your mind is focused on, is where your energy is going to go. That is the energy you are going to bring into your life."

Growing up, my mind was focused on not wanting to end up "just like my mother."

But, before she was diagnosed with schizophrenia, I

wanted to be just like her. She was beautiful. A cross between Audrey Hepburn, Barbara Streisand, and Olivia Newton-John. She would dance so elegantly for me in the living room when I was a child. My favorite dance was from the ballet *Coppélia*. The record had a picture of a woman in a ballet tutu, face painted like a doll, with a huge wind-up gear attached to her back. The choreography for this particular ballet was like a cartoon. It was like a classical ballet version of someone dancing "The Robot." I loved watching my mom dance for me.

We'd go to the movies together. We'd go to the mall and shop together. We'd pick out patterns at the fabric store and she would teach me how to sew. She taught me how to make scrambled eggs, grilled cheese sandwiches, and how to heat up Chef Boyardee raviolis. She would let me help her bake cakes and cookies from scratch and make Jell-O for dessert in different shapes and colors. When I was with my mother on her good days, I felt like the best version of myself.

Unfortunately, on her bad days, she was a far different person. She'd stay cloistered and alone in her room with the curtains drawn tight. So I learned to turn on the record player myself. I would sing and dance along to my mother's childhood *Mickey Mouse Club* records while she stayed in bed until noon.

My mother was in and out of the hospital for most of my childhood. She was impossible to keep up with because she would go missing every time she had a psychotic break. I watched friends of hers grow weary of her illness and they started to detach and disappear. This included my father.

Naturally, I assumed that if I grew up to be like my mother, people would stop loving me and I'd end up alone and ostracized, too. My friends' parents grew concerned about letting them play at my house. How could they be sure their kids were safe when my mother wasn't always all there?

True, she would sometimes sit and stare out the window in an odd way. Sure, she would sometimes say weird things that didn't make sense. No, she wasn't always in the mood to play with me and she would sleep in. Was that really all that bad? Who was she hurting? As a child, I didn't understand it at all.

When my mother was diagnosed with "Manic Depression" in the early 1970s, doctors still didn't have a good grasp on how to treat mental illness. My Aunt Hannelore cried at the dinner table when my dad first told her my mom had been diagnosed. She was a doctor herself. She was painfully aware that children growing up with a mentally ill parent often will have problems later in life themselves.

She said to my father, "I'm worried about Leslie."

She was right to worry.

Mid-1970s

When my mother was hospitalized after her second miscarriage, I understood that the baby died before he or she had been born. Contrary to what I was initially told, I was not going to have a little baby brother or sister after all.

But then every spring, she kept going to the hospital and I wasn't allowed to visit her. I had to sit in the lobby of the hospital in front of the gift shop by myself. I'd talk to the security guard at the front desk. He explained to me how the neon rainbow light in the window of the gift shop worked. How the tubes were filled with different gasses that would light up in different colors. He explained that yellow was a difficult color to create in neon, so they just painted one of the lights yellow.

My dad kept his promise. Since I behaved myself while waiting in the lobby and didn't give anyone working there any trouble, he bought me the Yorkshire terrier stuffed toy that I'd been admiring in the gift shop window. The song "Too Much Heaven" by the Bee Gees was on heavy rotation on all the radio stations during that time, and we'd sing along in the car together to and from the hospital.

Being raised in a religious home, I believed God was real. Yet I was always afraid of worshipping God the wrong way and pissing him off. Or worse, what if Satan was pretending to be God and I was worshipping Satan without knowing it? Praying and believing in Jesus with all my might, I hoped that someday my mom would be cured. But that day never came. As my eight-year-old mind tried to grasp the concept of praying to God, when my mother didn't get well, I wondered if, like dialing the wrong number on a telephone, I had accidentally spoken to the wrong god?

Every single spring, our lives and routines would be disrupted. Easter time was a trigger for my mother. She would remember her miscarriages, and everything would go to shit. Then she'd be hospitalized again. Since my mother had miscarried both her pregnancies after me, I am an only child. Whenever my mom was hospitalized, I was alone after school. Most of the time, I'd have to let myself into the house with a key around my neck. I'd watch *The Electric Company* on PBS and *Tom and Jerry* cartoons to keep myself company. Sometimes, I'd put records on and sing along. I'd record myself, then listen back, cringe at the bad notes, and then try singing the song again, over and over, until I was able to hit all the notes.

Sometimes, I stayed at my cousins' house while my mother was in the hospital. Other times, my dad would try to find a family friend to watch me after school or, if I was lucky, I'd get to stay with good friends of mine in the neighborhood. Sometimes I had to stay with friends of my parents that I didn't know all that well. I'd sit on the couch bored to tears while they watched the news. I'd hope that they wouldn't change the channel when *Little House on the Prairie* came on.

With the loss of my routine, my grades suffered. I'd fall

behind on schoolwork and struggle to pay attention in class. I was too worried about my mother being in the hospital, and sad knowing when I got off the school bus, no one would be home.

When things were going well in life, it was merely a sign that things would go to shit any minute. My mother would look happy, she'd be full of energy. The house would be spotless. Out of nowhere, she'd start saying stuff like "I don't need medication anymore, because Jesus cured me. He spoke to me. And the angels are speaking to me, too!"

Then she would stop taking her medications. Emotional drama would follow. Sometimes there were suicide attempts. Ultimately, she would end up back in the hospital. And when I was alone, I started having anxiety attacks.

The 1980s

My first anxiety attack happened after I went shopping with my parents one night. We were at the A&S department store in Paramus, New Jersey, and my dad was being fitted for a new suit for a business trip to Germany. In a display case in the front of the store were these adorable, collectable, and expensive Madame Alexander Dolls. My mother loved these dolls and asked my dad if they could buy me one. It was not my birthday, or Christmas. I hadn't even passed an important test or gotten an A+ on an assignment. My parents had wanted to buy me this gift "just because." So they let me pick one of them out. The doll I chose was "Beth" from Little Women. She had brunette hair, like mine, and wore a pink dress with a white pinafore.

I couldn't sleep when night fell. Absolute fear and terror came over me. I was sure that something awful was going to happen to make up for this doll my parents bought me. I didn't deserve it. I woke up in the middle of the night, and the panic attack started. I had to sleep on my parents' bedroom floor on a mat because I was freaking out so badly. Every time I thought about my beautiful brunette doll in her pink dress, the feeling of dread sharpened in my gut. I didn't have the heart to explain to my parents what their sweet gesture had stirred up inside me. I was a spoiled brat and felt guilty. I was going to have to "pay for this doll" in some way or form.

I believed I was not allowed to have good things without something bad happening.

And that wasn't the last time I experienced that feeling of dread. My dad bought me a surfboard for my seventeenth birthday. I'd been begging him for one ever since I had a crush on this surfer I met in Long Beach Island. He finally bought it for me. The same thing happened that night when I tried to sleep. I had an anxiety attack just like the one I had the night that my parents bought me the Madame Alexander Doll. Once again, I thought I didn't deserve the surfboard.

This carried over when I tried to learn to surf, too. I didn't do too bad the first couple of years I tried to learn to surf. I caught a few waves, learned to stand up, and even found myself surfing in November a few times in a full wetsuit.

There was always this nagging thought in the back of my head that said, "If you are too happy about stuff, you are going to have to pay for it. You may enjoy surfing now, but one day, you will drown for having the audacity to think you could be a surfer." It was only a matter of time before the other shoe dropped.

I must admit, the anxiety I had when I was first learning to ride a motorcycle wasn't much different from my adolescent panic on the surfboard. I no longer believed that I would be "punished" by karma for trying to learn to ride a motorcycle. I found myself second guessing whether I was capable of learning how to ride without simultaneously having an anxiety attack and hurting myself. The bottom line was, I still didn't trust myself.

Instead of focusing on the things I wanted to become in life, I only noticed the things I was afraid of and wanted to avoid. I didn't want to be diagnosed with depression or any other mental illness. I didn't want to ever have to take medications, and I didn't want people to abandon me when I was having a mental crisis. I didn't want people to think I was weird and leave me.

These fears first started to manifest in junior high. It's okay to be weird and quirky when you are a kid, until you hit puberty. Then all of the sudden, kids who used to be your best friends become super judgmental about everything, labelling what seemed like random things as cool or uncool. I couldn't keep up with it. Girls I was friends with prior to that drifted away from me.

High school was even worse. I'd gone to the same school from nursery school until eighth grade, and I knew everyone like family. I felt accepted by the kids I'd grown up with since age five, for the most part. But when I went off to high school, I hardly knew anyone.

That's when I started to notice that I wasn't processing the world like everyone else. I wasn't around people I'd grown up with, who were comfortable with how quirky I was. These new kids didn't know my past, and the struggles I'd had with my mom, the way the kids I'd grown up with did. These new kids at this new school did not know me from Adam. Therefore, they had no empathy. I was perfect fodder for bullies because I was so socially awkward.

Spring 1985

Catholic schoolgirls are the worst. Honestly, I don't know how I survived it. I just wanted to be left alone. I tried as best I could to mind my own business, but I did manage to make two friends during my freshman year in high school, Liz and Diane.

Diane had a crush on a boy that was dating this super popular girl, Jenny, who took the same school bus as I did. Diane and I met him when we were at the all-boys school trying out for the Varsity cheerleading squad. I had no interest in cheerleading. I just wanted to meet boys and have a social life. There were weeks when the only males I saw were my dad, my math teacher, and the paperboy.

So, after cheerleading tryouts ended, Diane and I were waiting in front of the all-boys school for my mom to pick us up. There was this guy (who we will just refer to as A for "Asshole") milling around with his friends. He came over to us and made small talk. He asked if we had tried out for cheerleading. He was kind of hitting on my friend Diane, but I noticed that he had a necklace on with half a gold heart hanging from the chain.

"Who has the other half of your heart?" I interrupted the flirting to ask.

"My what? Oh. This? Ehh, this is nothing. Do you know Jenny Moyer?" A asked.

"Oh yes. Jenny and I are on the same school bus. I know her."

"Yeah, she was my girlfriend, but she got fat and she dyed her hair, and now it looks purple. I don't know why she did that."

He continued talking shit about Jenny and was simultaneously telling Diane how hot he thought she was. Diane had big boobs. My chest was concave.

I heard myself asking out loud, "Why are you talking about your girlfriend like that?"

For some reason, Diane was still interested in this A, even after he shit-talked about the girl who gave him half a gold heart. Diane wanted me to find out if Jenny was still dating him and if they were going to the spring dance together.

So, the next day on the bus, Jenny was talking to her friends and was describing a lavender tulle dress. She said she was practicing walking around her house wearing tube socks in a pair of silver stilettos to stretch them out. She was planning on wearing the sparkly footwear with the poufy lavender dress (after all, this was the 1980s, and everything was over the top).

So I figured it was the perfect time to ask her, "Oh, are you going to the spring dance?"

"Yes! I am," she answered brightly. "Are you going to go?"

"Ah, probably not. I don't know anyone to ask to go with me. Who are you taking?"

"I'm going with A."

"Oh, I thought so. I met him when I was waiting for my mom to pick me up after cheerleading tryouts the other day."

And just to be sure she knew I wasn't trying to hit on her boyfriend, I said, "I saw the heart necklace you gave him. I love that. So cute! I bet you guys are just the cutest couple ever. Take pictures so we can all see your dress!"

I didn't feel the need to tell Jenny how her boyfriend had been shit-talking about her hair. Or how he said she was getting fat. I wasn't trying to hurt anyone's feelings. I was just sleuthing for Diane. That happened on a Friday. I called up Diane and told her the bad news. I didn't give it another thought for the rest of the weekend. But, the following Monday, when I got on the school bus, bagels with cream cheese were getting hurled at my head.

"What is going on?" I asked, annoyed. Jenny Moyer and her friends were throwing balled-up pieces of paper and their breakfast at me.

"You know what you did to Jenny, you bitch!" one of Jenny's friends, who I didn't know and never said two words to, barked at me.

When we arrived at school, Jenny informed me why everyone hated my guts. Turns out that A said that I had called Jenny fat and said she had purple hair. Basically, everything that A had said about Jenny when he was flirting with Diane, he turned around and told Jenny I'd said them.

"Jenny, I never said those things about you."

"Are you calling my boyfriend a liar?"

"Well, yes. If he told you I said those things, then he is a liar."

"Fuck you! Bitch! Don't call my boyfriend a liar!" She threw an empty milk carton at my head.

"Yeah, fuck you! Don't call her boyfriend a liar!" a chorus of her minions repeated.

"Why did you think that A would be interested in a stupid kid like you?" Jenny mocked.

Ouch. Jenny hit me where it hurt. When I was fourteen years old, but I still looked about twelve and I knew it. I had not broken 100 pounds on the scale yet; my 5'1" frame was holding steady at 92 pounds. I could still shop in the pre-teen section, had zero curves, and was wearing a training bra with a triple-A cup. I had to roll up my plaid Catholic uniform skirt so it wouldn't fall down around my ankles when I walked up the stairs. Eighth grade boys hit on me all the time. The juniors and seniors thought I was still in grammar school.

Jenny and her crew basically made the remainder of my freshman year a living hell. They made bets about who could make me cry first. They spat spitballs at me during religion class, taunted me in the cafeteria when I was trying to do my homework, and even harassed me during Catholic Mass in the auditorium. What nice, sweet Catholic Christian girls they were.

Luckily, I didn't make the Varsity cheerleading squad that all the popular (mean) girls were on. That just would have given them more opportunities to berate me. However, I did make Junior Varsity at the OTHER all-boys school, far away from Jenny and her nasty friends.

But the energy that I wanted to get away from followed me, because once again, I was thinking about what I didn't want, instead of what I wanted. I didn't want to be a bully like Jenny and her friends. I didn't want to associate with any of them.

So on the junior varsity squad, far away from Jenny and her clan, we were voting on which of us should be captain and co-captain. My friends and I were convinced that our friend Liz would make co-captain. However, we were surprised when Maggie, the daughter of our coach, was announced as co-captain. Liz and Diane, very quietly and inconspicuously, were asking everyone in our group of friends who they voted for.

Unfortunately, I have a big loud voice that carries. And even though I was trying to whisper, Maggie and her friends overheard me ask Liz and Diane, "Wait, what are you guys saying? Do you think Maggie only made co-captain because her mom is the coach? Who voted for *her*?"

I looked across the room. Maggie had heard me and was crying. Then Liz started crying.

Great. I had become exactly what I hated. A bitchy cheerleader, like Jenny and her friends.

I had put so much energy into thinking about who I didn't want to be like. I had forgotten to focus on the kind of person I wanted to be. And now I was a bully, too.

By the spring of my sophomore year, I ended up quitting cheerleading. It was never my "thing" to begin with. There had to be a better way to create a social life.

Instead, I took a job at the movie theater in town ringing up popcorn, sodas, and candy, and started to create a social life for myself there. That summer, I spent my days and evenings working with the other kids, discussing our favorite movies, the best beach towns to go on vacation, the state of the dried-up hotdogs on the snack bar grill, and which town had the best Fourth of July fireworks. It was a nice escape from the bullying I was enduring in high school. I preferred their company; these kids were nerdy, nonjudgmental, and genuinely nice. They loved *Star Wars* and video games and

Dungeons and Dragons. I met some boys while working at the movie theater, and even went on some dates.

Dating turned out to be just one more thing that was awkward and scary for me. I'd meet a guy. We'd hang out with each other for a few weeks. But I would often feel so anxious and scared about being rejected, that I would end up sabotaging things. I had to break up with them before they broke up with me. Or before I got attached to them. I'd find an excuse. Like, he didn't call me exactly when he said he would. He showed up at my house twenty minutes late. He looked at me the wrong way. Or maybe he didn't look at me at all and was looking at another girl. Or whatever it was that made me feel insecure in whatever moment I was in. I'd get so anxious I'd almost be dizzy, then I'd react by cutting them off.

This is how I ended up doing relationships for most of my young adult life. I would find myself looking in the wrong direction. I kept thinking how I didn't want to be vulnerable, instead of thinking, "I want to find love." After I would end things, I'd spend the next six months (or even longer), pining away over them in absolute agony. I'd be wishing they'd call me and beg me to come back. Preferably while holding up a boom-box blasting "In Your Eyes." My suffering was real, even though I had been the one to end things.

March 2006

When I met Mark, I made a promise to myself that I would not treat things the same way I had treated other relationships. I was not going to second guess things, or end things just because I was scared. I was not going to rush things. I was not going to break up with him just because I feared he might break up with me first. I was not going to try to turn things into an unrealistic fairy tale. I was not going to sabotage anything, no matter how afraid I was.

In other words, I was focused on a lot of things I did not

want to do in that relationship, rather than focusing on what I did want to do. I wanted to enjoy the process of getting to know Mark, but it's hard to do that when you have a list full of don'ts hanging over your head.

I met Mark long after I had graduated high school and college, and years after I'd finally learned what codependence was from Matty. We met right after my second hospitalization, where I'd attempted to saw my wrists with a sharpened plastic knife.

I met Mark on social media immediately after spending the weekend in the psychiatric unit.

Mark was a bright spot for me. Bored at work and surfing around the internet, I came across Mark's profile picture. It was the lead character in one of my favorite comedies, Lumbergh from the movie *Office Space*. So, I just kind of impulsively and randomly sent him a message saying, *"OMG, I love that movie! It's so funny!"* He sent me a friend request. The first photo of his that caught my eye, was a picture of him and his daughter. He's wearing jeans and a T-shirt with a genuine smile on his face. She looks about six or seven years old and is a miniature blonde version of him, with long wavy hair and big, beautiful eyes. In the photo, she is sitting on his shoulders wearing a pink sundress and fancy cowboy boots. I immediately fell in love with both of them.

We chatted over social media for about two days and then Mark sent me a message asking, "When are we going out for a bevvy?"

One Wednesday night, we met up for happy hour in Venice Beach at a rooftop bar. As soon as I recognized him from his photo, I thought, "Be careful with this one." I don't know why I thought that. Be careful not to hurt him? Or myself?

He thanked me for looking like my profile picture, then told me some funny internet dating stories about women who looked nothing like their profile pictures. At one point, I had excused myself to go to the bathroom, and when I came back, there was some girl with a drink in her hand talking to Mark. She looked over at me and smiled, then introduced herself.

"Hi, I'm Michelle!" She smiled at me, holding an empty drink and cigarette in one hand, and extending the other hand to shake mine.

"Lola," I said, giving her my nickname.

Then she said, "I'll be right back. I need a refill," before walking to the bar.

"Who is that?" I asked Mark.

"I have no idea. She asked me if you were my girlfriend and said she'd like to come home with both of us. Does this happen to you often?"

"Uh, no. First time. You?"

"Uhhhh, nope. Can't say that it has."

We politely turned Michelle down when she came back.

We ate, drank, and laughed, then watched the sunset from the rooftop until the bartender made the last call, and then I brought Mark home with me.

I was excited the next day. Maybe this guy could be my next boyfriend. My friend Andy was living down the road from me in Venice at the time. We had dated briefly a few years earlier, but now we were really good friends. We have the same birthday and would often celebrate together. I stopped by Andy's apartment to tell him about my awesome date , and how I hoped he would invite me on a second date.

"Lola," Andy said, calling me by my nickname as if he were about to scold me. "Did you sleep with him on the first date?"

"Uh, yeah. Why?"

"I thought you said you weren't going to rush things?" He shook his head.

"Well, he will definitely call you for a second date, because he knows he's guaranteed to get laid a second time." Andy laughed.

Mark did call me for a second date. As well as a third, and then a fourth.

I still didn't know what a normal relationship was supposed to look like, but this seemed easy enough. Even though we were both struggling financially at the time, it seemed we were managing to have fun anyway. We were laughing about our problems together because there was nothing left to do but laugh. Or so I thought.

Mark was in sales and had a commission-based salary. He said he had been making a killing until recently. The economy had started crashing. Los Angeles was affected about two years before the rest of the country was hit. Now Mark was finding that his bank accounts were dwindling, downplaying how much trouble he was in.

Mark and I talked regularly, but he didn't call me non-stop. Sometimes I wouldn't hear from him for a few days after we hung out, but I decided not to worry about it too much. I was flirting with, and occasionally hanging out with, a couple other guys I had met online. In particular, I was indulging in a groupie crush I had on Baby Paul Cullen, one of the Z-Boys from Dogtown—those guys who invented modern skateboarding in the 1970s during a drought in Southern California. He had slipped into my DMs a couple times, and we'd been on a few dates. When I was honest with myself, though, I had to admit that I didn't have feelings for him the way I did for Mark.

I genuinely only wanted to be with Mark, but I hated to admit it. Feeling uncomfortably vulnerable, I figured I'd better keep my options open.

Mark happened to be one of the first guys I dated during the early days of social media. A new dating dilemma had arisen. There were way too many leggy blonde women on Mark's social media page, and I had no idea who any of them were. Ex-girlfriends? Old friends from high school? Fuckbuddies? Coworkers? His sisters? This was way more information than I needed. I had no idea if any of these airbrushed women were a threat, but I certainly felt inferior to all of them. By the looks of his social media page, it seemed like he had a thing for tall, well-polished blondes who worked in finance or real estate and probably went to spin class after shopping at Whole Foods Market. I was a short, messy brunette barely making it as a secretary and dispensary worker, going to a donation-based yoga class, and shopping for groceries at the 99-cent store.

One night, Mark and I went out for happy hour at a bar that was owned by Arnold Schwarzenegger, and met up with his friend Randy. The drinks and food during happy hour were so ridiculously cheap and right in our budget. It's no wonder that the place went out of business a few years later.

I excused myself to go to the bathroom. The Z-Boy texted me while I was in there, asking me if I wanted to go out with him the next day. I was hoping to bring Mark home with me that night, so I texted the Z-Boy back that I wasn't sure if I was going to be available, but I'd let him know.

After I went back to the bar, Randy was there, but Mark was gone. I thought maybe he went to smoke a cigarette outside or was in the bathroom. I asked Randy where he went.

"He left. I'm so mad at him. I told him to wait for you. Asshole," Randy said angrily. But I honestly thought he was joking and laughed. I sat down to sip on my rum and coke.

After about ten minutes, and still no Mark, I asked again, "Seriously, Randy, where the hell did Mark go? Is he vomiting in the bathroom or something?"

"No," Randy said with a scowl on his face, "Mark left. He got a phone call from his ex-wife. I don't know what the fuck she said to him, but he was really upset. Like, furious. I told him to calm down and wait for you. He got impatient though. He called a cab and left."

"Wait, I thought you were kidding. Are you serious?"

"Yes, I'm serious. I've been trying to tell you."

I ran outside to the parking lot and saw that Mark's truck was still there. I called him on my cell phone, but he didn't pick up. I texted him—he didn't answer.

Honestly, I wasn't even pissed at Mark for leaving, just worried. Who leaves someone at a bar in a bathroom like that? We hadn't been arguing. He hadn't hinted he was upset with me. Something bad must have happened during that phone call with his ex-wife.

I texted him, "Hey, are you okay? Why did you leave?

No response.

So I started calling him.

He wouldn't pick up.

Finally, figuring I had nothing to lose, I left him a message asking him why he'd left. I told him I wasn't mad, I was more worried, because it's not normal to just leave someone you're getting along perfectly fine with in the bathroom, without even a text or explanation. Was he upset with me? If so, I felt he owed it to me to let me know what he was angry about.

At some point, we did end up talking on the phone. I don't know if he finally gave in and picked up, or if he'd listened to my message and called me back, but he said something along the lines of, "I don't really want to talk about it, let's just forget everything, okay? It's not going to work."

"Okay, if that's what you really want, but can you tell me what I did wrong? I think you owe it to me to let me know, so I don't make the same mistake with someone else."

I knew damn well I hadn't actually done anything to deserve to be left in the bathroom and wasn't going to let him off the hook.

Mark let out an exasperated sigh. Then he said, "My ex-wife called me when you were in the bathroom., and she pissed me off. And you were taking fucking forever in there. So I got annoyed and just left."

"You were mad at your ex-wife, so you left me in the bathroom without even sending a text?"

Then the truth started to come out. He explained, "My ex just told me she quit her job and left Los Angeles for a good for job on the East Coast, and she took my daughter with her."

"Oh my god, that's awful," I said, sincerely shocked and frustrated for him.

"She told me I'm never going to see my daughter again. If she thinks I'm going to let that happen, she's out of her mind. Now I'm going to need a lawyer, which is going to cost me." He had already admitted to me that his finances were tight, so I knew this was the last thing he needed.

Mark and I continued to see each other for the next five months. It was obvious by his social media page that he was seeing other girls, too.

Trying not to think about it, I'd call up the Z-Boy to distract myself when Mark wasn't around. He was a fun distraction for a while. Until, that is, he got a call while we were at the movies and found out his ex-girlfriend was going to have his baby. (He ended up getting back together with his ex-girlfriend, Christie Martin, who is such a cool person, and a talented jewelry designer and real estate agent to boot. They had a daughter. She and I are still friends on social media today.)

One afternoon, Mark and I met up at Finn McCool's on Main Street in Santa Monica for lunch. He was standing outside, smoking a cigarette and talking to his father on his cell phone. He informed me that his father and I had a common interest in astrology. Gushing all over my astrological connections with Mark to his dad, I told him, "My Jupiter is in Mark's seventh house conjunct his Sun, and his moon is conjunct my Sun." I giggled, as these were considered auspicious connections for a relationship, astrologically speaking.

"Well, did you notice how Uranus is cazimi his Sun in his relationship house, though?" His father pointed out a configuration usually associated with fear of commitment. Like, panic attack–level anxiety around commitment and responsibilities. But you know me. I only see what I want to see. Plus, the relationship house in my astrological chart was almost as scary as Mark's anyway. If not worse. Astrologically speaking.

"That configuration could also be a surprising friendship!" I pointed out, hopeful.

One day while I was at work, I got an email from Mark asking if I wanted to make plans for the entire weekend. He said he had the following weekend free and wanted to make me dinner and then maybe go out and see my friend Danielle spin at a club in Chinatown.

When he arrived at my apartment that Friday night, he said he needed to talk to me. Then he confessed that he'd been dating other girls and apologized, which actually made me laugh. "Duh, obviously," I said. "I didn't realize that you were trying to keep that a secret from me, but okay. Apology accepted."

In Chinatown, my friends had taken over the club and decorated it with big red fake mushrooms under hot-pink lights. Garden gnomes were scattered everywhere. My friend Danielle is a DJ, and she and some of my other friends were spinning house music. Girls were walking around dressed as fairies, and everything was pink, red, and glittery. High on ecstasy, we danced all night. We almost took a fairy home with us for a threesome, but then decided against it.

Saturday morning, we slept in, then went back down to Venice Beach and had mimosas at brunch. I ran into some friends at the restaurant who told me, "He is, like, the most normal guy we have ever seen you with. Are you finally in a normal relationship?"

I thought so.

We hit a dive bar later that night and played pool. Yet another woman tried to get us to take her home with us. Mark asked me, "Are you sure this never happened to you before? 90

percent of the time we hang out, some woman is trying to come home with us. This is, like, very odd."

"Honest to god, Mark, I only seem to get hit on by other women when I'm with you. I have no clue what is going on."

To this day, I still can't explain it. Never happened with any other guys I dated before him. Never happened with any other guys I dated after him.

On the way home, we stopped at Gelson's, a very exclusive and expensive grocery store, where Mark bought a couple of expensive certified Angus beef filet mignons. Then we went back to Mark's sister's house, where he and his daughter had been living since he realized he could no longer afford his apartment. She and the family were gone for the weekend. Mark grilled the filets for us for dinner, then we went skinny dipping in the pool out back. After our romantic swim was over and I'd showered, I walked around the house looking for Mark. The energy seemed to have shifted and the house seemed strangely quiet. I walked around the house looking for Mark and found him lying on his daughter's twin-sized bed, curled up on his side. There was a spiral-bound notebook that he was writing in. He closed it and put it into the nightstand drawer and settled his head back onto the pillow.

"Is this where you want to sleep tonight?" I asked. He nodded yes. He looked so sad. So, I crawled into his daughter's twin-sized bed with him, and we fell asleep spooning for a moment, but then Mark sat up and said he wanted to go back to my place because he wasn't sure what time his sister was getting back. We went back to my place and fell asleep in the living room while binge-watching DVD's of *Freaks and Geeks*.

A calm quiet fell over me as we dozed off on the couch. Maybe things weren't perfect. Maybe we were both still struggling to heal. Mark's pain over his daughter was almost palpable, and it made me hurt so much for him. But when we fell asleep next to each other that way, I felt so settled inside. I thought, "This is exactly what I've always wanted."

The next morning, we strolled around Santa Monica and Venice with my pit bull, Phoebe. We grabbed some burgers on the outdoor patio at the Firehouse Grill. Then, after we went back to my place, I played my guitar at my apartment and sang while he smoked a cigarette. And then it was time to go. Mark said he had to work in the morning, and so did I. He desperately needed to make a sale. He kept stalling before he left. He sat down on the floor for a few minutes to pet Phoebe.

After much procrastination, Mark finally got up to leave. But, before he left my apartment, he stopped in the doorway, turned around, paused, and looked me straight in the eyes. He put his hand on my shoulder and gave me what seemed like the saddest look. I thought he was going to say something important, but then he just hugged me, walked out the door, and drove away.

I wondered, "What did that look mean?"

For a split moment, I found myself feeling the same way I felt when my mother gave me permission to sleep over at my friend Kathy's house on a school night. Like, something was off. Thoughts like these came frequently when I was dating someone who I really liked. I was always paranoid when things seemed to be going well; I thought the shit was going to hit the fan any minute. I quickly brushed those thoughts away from my mind. Refusing to read into it, I convinced myself that he was just sad that our weekend had come to an end. After all, I was sad the weekend had come to an end, so why wouldn't he be? I was finally in what my friends called "the most normal-looking relationship they ever saw me in." I wasn't going to jinx it.

After he left, though, I couldn't stop thinking about "the look" he'd given me. I considered driving past his apartment but quickly talked myself out of it.

"Don't be a psycho girlfriend. Don't be paranoid. Don't go stalking him. That's just crazy. Don't look for a reason to break up with him just because you feel vulnerable. Don't assume whenever things are good, there is something bad lurking around the corner. Don't sabotage this."

Then, when I didn't hear from Mark for a week, the wind was taken out of my sails. I ate a pint of double chocolate chip Haagen-Dazs while listening to the song "Protection" by Massive Attack on repeat. I was afraid to contact him because I didn't want to confirm whether or not I was actually being ghosted. Maybe he was busy with legal stuff and his daughter. Maybe he was running errands. Maybe he was babysitting his niece for his sister. I didn't have a good feeling about it, though. Everything had seemed so perfect. And now I was back to thinking, "I knew it was too good to be true."

Then one day over a week later, I came home after work, and was surprised to see Mark was sitting in his truck parked outside of my apartment.

"Hey," he said nervously. "I'm sorry I'm just showing up like this unannounced. I couldn't pay my cell phone bill and so I—that's why I haven't called you all week. Is it okay that I'm here?"

OMG. Was it okay? Are you kidding? I was thrilled to have him just show up like that.

"Hey…." I said somewhat casually, trying to hide my utter enthusiasm. "My phone was actually turned off because I couldn't pay my bill either."

"Come in and have dinner," I continued, still hiding my sheer delight. I couldn't wait to make him a grilled cheese sandwich.

"Thank you so much for that," Mark said after eating the cheddar and mozzarella on sourdough that I'd made him. "It really hit the spot." He asked if he could stay over, saying he thought maybe his sister and her husband could use a night without him there. He'd leave early for work in the morning. That was fine by me.

The next night when I got home from work, Mark was sitting in his truck parked outside of my apartment again.

"Hi," he said, looking somewhat embarrassed. "Is it okay that I'm here again? I still haven't gotten my phone turned back on, so that's why I didn't call." He laughed. I wondered for a second why he hadn't called me from his office, or wherever it is that he worked? But I convinced myself it was probably because they had a strict policy about personal phone calls.

This went on for about a week or two. So happy to have him showing up at my place every night, and not wanting to jinx it, I didn't dare ask him if there was something else going on. A couple times, I came home from my job to find Mark still at my apartment. It was obvious he hadn't gone to work.

"Oh, I decided to skip the office and send out some resumes. I need a supplementary income. The stock market is tanking."

"Okay, I'll take it. Sounds like a good enough excuse to me," I thought. Anytime I'd get the feeling that there was more going on than I was seeing, I'd just push it out of my mind.

Then one day, I came home from work and my apartment was spotless. Absolutely spotless. Mark looked embarrassed. He had been at my apartment all day. Said he cooked himself lunch, then started washing dishes. The next thing he knew, he had cleaned my entire kitchen. Including the grout in the tiles. He said he wasn't even thinking, and moved onto the bathroom, and had bleached the toilet, the tub, the shower curtain. And then the living room. All the dog hair had been vacuumed away. The messy blankets that had been strewn about the couch and futon were now folded neatly. My walk-in closet was color coordinated and everything. My shoes were lined up like soldiers.

I always had trouble staying on top of shit. I hated that I had a hard time keeping my place clean and organized. This was like a dream. My apartment looked like it belonged to a grown woman instead of a sloppy teenager. I walked around my apartment stunned at how shiny and incredible everything looked.

"Oh my god, you cleaned my house?!" I heard my voice go up an octave.

"I know…it was intrusive of me…I'm so sorry. I was cooking, then I did some dishes, and then I started cleaning. I just kept going…"

"My closet looks amazing."

"You're not mad?" Mark looked worried.

"Mad? Are you kidding? My apartment looks incredible!"

"I feel like I violated your privacy, kind of…"

"Okay." I put my purse down and looked at him. He was sitting in my doorway drinking a diet Coke.

"What is going on? So, like, either you are madly in love with me and want to run away to Vegas and get married right now. Or is something else going on with you? This just seems too good to be true. Please don't tell me you're, like, dying of AIDS or cancer or something…"

"I've been lying to you." He cut me off.

My stomach dropped.

"I've been lying to my sister," his voice began to shake. "I've been lying to my friends, everyone."

I started to get scared.

"I haven't been working. I haven't made a sale in over a year. I quit the company I was working for because I wasn't making any money. I thought I was going to be able to find another job right away, but I haven't."

Things were actually a lot worse than he had been telling me.

"I've been going to the library every day and applying for jobs, telling my family and friends that I was going to work. But, over the last six months, I've lost everything. I lost my apartment. I had to sell my classic baby-blue Thunderbird and buy this dumb truck. After I couldn't pay rent anymore and had to move in with my sister and her family, I just felt like such a burden. And I've been so stressed out, I completely forgot to pay for my storage unit, and I lost all my stuff. Photos of my daughter when she was a baby, and a bunch of other sentimental things. Gone."

"When I couldn't find a job, for a while, I thought about joining the Army. Figured I'd go to Iraq. Thinking if I died there, my daughter would be set for life. But then I thought, what if I don't get killed there but end up with a permanent disability instead? Plus, I'm a Democrat and I don't even support the war. I hate George W. Bush," he said as he threw down his cigarette and snuffed it out.

"So, I pretty much was feeling done with it all at that point. And then I met you, and we were having a great time together," he said.

"But I was lying to you about just how bad things were. The night when my ex-wife called and told me she took my daughter out of the state and started this custody battle, I lost it. She knew it was going to financially kill me, since I was going to have to hire a lawyer. She threatened me and said I would never see my daughter again.

"After that, I was just done. I was done.

"Then, just when I thought it couldn't get worse, my truck got broken into when I was at your apartment a few nights ago. They stole my laptop computer and my CD player."

Mark continued, "So I stole my brother-in-law's jars of quarters and cashed them in so I could take you out for the weekend, make you an awesome dinner. I just wanted us to have a good time together before I...." He interrupted himself.

"So, I just decided I was done. Done. After we spent the weekend together, I went home. I had written a four-page letter in a notebook I left in my daughter's nightstand telling her how much I love her. I filled up both cars in the garage with gas. I put NPR on the radio. Then I took a bottle of sleeping pills, downed them with two bottles of vodka, and went to sleep.

"I woke up the next morning without so much as a headache. Both cars were out of gas. I pushed my truck down the hill and hid it around the block so my sister would think I went to work. Then I ended up wandering around the Westside of Los Angeles all week, crashing at different friends' houses after happy hour, until I ran out of people to crash with."

"I managed to sneak onto the roof of a building in Century City and thought about jumping. But chickened out."

Chills ran down my spine. Mark kept talking.

"So, I finally scraped enough money together to put some gas in my truck, drove over here, and I've been with you ever since. I can't face my sister, my family. I'm so mad at myself. I'm embarrassed. And I need your advice. I don't know what to tell my sister about why I stole those quarters."

My heart was shattered. All this time I'd been feeling so happy, so thrilled to have this guy coming around. I'd been suicidal before I met him and felt like maybe we had something worth living for together. I felt guilty for not realizing how much trouble he had been in. How did I miss this?

And here he was, worried about the quarters he stole from his brother-in-law. That was the least of his problems.

"Mark, you have to tell your sister the truth. Nothing else is going to make sense to her about your actions. You need to be honest and ask for her help and support. You should see a therapist. Maybe go on an antidepressant. You need to be strong for your daughter."

His daughter.

For a minute, all the painful memories from my own childhood came rushing back. I remembered how much it hurt when my mom tried to commit suicide. I'd felt so rejected by her, and so vulnerable. On her good days, my mother could make me feel like the best version of myself. On her bad days,

I wondered why I hadn't been able to make her feel the same way? And now, I was feeling that way about Mark. Like I'd somehow failed him because I hadn't been able to make him feel like life wasn't so bad, the way he had done for me. At the same time, I wanted to scold him, but I couldn't. He felt bad enough already. It was a stupid thing to do, and he already knew that. He didn't need me to rub it in. I was going to bury my own feelings. He didn't need to be burdened with my emotions on top of his own problems.

I decided to take a shower so I could cry without him seeing me. When it hit me how close he'd come to dying, I nearly collapsed inside. I must have been in the shower for a long time, because Mark came into the bathroom to see if I was okay.

"So, was everything that happened between us a lie?" I asked through tears I hoped he couldn't see, as the water from the shower ran down my face.

I had so many emotions: anger, guilt, shame, heartbreak. I wanted to support him, but I was being triggered right back to an old state of mind. I was ten years old again, listening to my mother tell me she wanted to die. I'd felt like I wasn't worth living for. I was feeling helpless, powerless. Here, I'd forced myself not to second guess my happiness with Mark. But I had been right to.

"No, it wasn't a lie. I really wanted you to be the last person I was with…."

Mark paused for a moment.

"I wanted you to be the last person I was with before I died."

That made me cry even more. Then Mark tried to be strong.

"Come on. Get out of the shower. You're over-reacting. Everything is going to be okay."

"Okay? It's going to be okay? You almost died!" I bawled.

Mark asked if he could stay with me for a few more days

and then he would tell his sister everything. He just wasn't ready to go home.

"Do you want me to leave?" he asked.

"You can stay as long as you need to."

I didn't want him to leave. Ever.

The next day, I walked to work. My car had broken down, and I didn't have enough money to fix it. Luckily, my job was less than two miles from my apartment. I wore my heels at my desk, then ran home to Mark in my sneakers.

Looking down at the cracks in the sidewalk, I found myself jumping over them the way I had when I was a child. Back when my mother had tried to commit suicide. Back when I was afraid of finding my mother dead at home.

I stopped dead in my tracks when I realized what I was doing. I burst into tears and started thanking God, if there was a God, for not letting Mark die. I didn't know why that night in the garage hadn't killed him, but I was so grateful it hadn't. When I finally pulled myself together, I stood up and walked home. Smiling for Mark when I walked in the door, I pushed my heartbreak all the way down, as far down as I could. That night, I slept with my arms wrapped tightly around him.

Mark finally told his sister everything. She wanted him to come back to their house so she could be there for him. I got an email from Mark a few days later. His daughter was back in town for a dance recital of some kind. Mark had been there. He told me how proud he was of her, and how life was worth living. Especially for his daughter. How he must have been crazy to think she would have been better off without him.

"She is such an amazing kid. How could I have ever thought of leaving her? I love my daughter so much. I'm fighting for full custody."

I adored this man.

But I was triggered back into that fight or flight response that I lived in as a child.

That quiet, settled feeling I'd had with him days earlier was gone, and there was nothing I could do to bring us back to that place. There was no more responding to my relationship with Mark. Just emotional reactions to my fears that he might disappear on me without an explanation. Being in a state of panic became my baseline normal with Mark.

I knew I would be setting him up for failure if I tried to pursue a relationship with him. He didn't have much left to give me, and I understood that. And quite honestly, I didn't have much to give him, either. I was too emotionally unstable myself. I was too insecure. Every time I found myself looking at the gorgeous blondes all over Mark's social media page, I felt inferior. He deserved a strong, smart, successful, hot woman. I felt like I was nothing but a hot mess. I wished I was more like what I believed the women on his social media page were like: financially stable and emotionally secure. Then I could just let him move in with me so I could take care of him. But I was financially unstable and emotionally insecure.

I knew just how badly Mark was struggling to make ends meet now. And I knew every last bit of time, money, and energy he had was going to go to his daughter, just as it should have been. I remembered what it was like in my own life. I had been raised by a single father from age fifteen on.

After my parents split up when I was fifteen, my mother was institutionalized in Arkansas. My father, still in New Jersey, started dating a woman he'd met on a business trip who lived in Maryland, three states away. He left me alone every single weekend to be with her. Many times, I'd sleep over at friends' homes. Their parents would look at me with pity in their eyes when I'd tell them my father was at his girlfriend's house for the weekend, again. Sometimes, I just couldn't stand to have the grown-ups look at me that way. So I'd lie and say my father was home when he wasn't. Because I was alone and too young to drive. I was isolated. I would often have anxiety attacks when I was alone. But my dad and his girlfriend accused me of being dramatic. They said I was overreacting.

Mark would never choose anyone over his daughter. He would never leave his girl alone to have an anxiety attack the way my father had. Every time I'd see him post pictures on social media of him and his daughter together on social media, it only made me love and respect him more. He was the kind of father I'd want raising my daughters, if I was ever lucky enough to have daughters of my own someday. Ironically, this was also the reason I couldn't be with him. Especially since I was still working the cannabis dispensary part time after work, trying to save up for nursing school. The last thing Mark needed was for his ex-wife to get wind that he was even just casually dating someone who sold weed at a dispensary. It would be ammunition for her to get full custody. There was no way I was going to even risk putting that kind of burden on him.

The last thing I wanted to do was to end things with Mark, the way I had ended many relationships in the past. When I was younger, I would end things with guys I was dating because I was scared, even when I really hadn't wanted to. I had to break it off with Mark, even though I really didn't want to. But this time, it wasn't because I was scared. It wasn't because I wanted to dump him before he had a chance to dump me, or to run away before I risked getting too attached. It wasn't because I felt inferior to the blonde women all over his social media page. It was because I genuinely cared about him too much to use him as a "drug," the way my codependent self was accustomed to. Not to mention, I couldn't afford to quit my job at the dispensary and felt I couldn't protect him and his daughter from that either.

So I sent him an email friend-zoning him, and I'm sure he was relieved that I was the one to do it. As much as I didn't want to end things, I knew I was setting myself up (and possibly him as well) for heartbreak, failure, and resentment if I didn't.

Mark and I hadn't been looking in the direction we wanted to go when we met. We were looking behind us, trying to run away from our mistakes.

June 2021

In motorcycle riding, there is a dangerous, potentially deadly phenomenon known as target fixation. It's considered a reaction to panic. More specifically, it is when you are literally looking in the direction you do NOT want to go, instead of the direction you do want to go.

On a motorcycle, target fixation happens when you are focusing on something that you don't want to hit, and ultimately, end up hitting it because you're focused on it. I once saw a motorcyclist run right off the road and into a pole, and there was barely a curve in the road. He was so busy looking at the pole on the side of the road, he hit it.

When you're on a motorcycle, wherever you are looking is where the bike will go. If you want to make a tight turn, you have to turn your head all the way, and look into that turn. If you look down, the bike will go down. If you look at a van parked on the side of the road, the motorcycle will head right for it.

The same is true in life. If we are focused on avoiding the things in life we are afraid of, or what we don't want in life, we are guaranteed to bring that energy we are trying to avoid into our life.

I had a yoga teacher in Santa Monica named Travis Eliot who would always say, "Where the mind goes is where the energy flows." I find this to be true both while riding a motorcycle and in life.

My husband came home from work the other day and complained, "I hate my job. I'm doing the exact opposite of what I wanted to do. I didn't want to sit in Los Angeles traffic for work, and I didn't want to work alone, and now all I do is drive around in Los Angeles traffic by myself."

My husband had taken a job with a motorcycle dealership in Orange County delivering motorcycles to people from San Diego all the way up to Fresno. His job required him to sit in traffic for hours at a time, alone.

My husband's mistake in his job search was focusing on what he didn't want, instead of what he wanted. He wanted to work for a motorcycle company, but he hadn't been clear in his mind about what he pictured himself doing on a daily basis.

Our brains cannot comprehend the word "no." There is no visual in our mind's eye for the words "no and don't." So if you say, "I don't want to forget my yoga mat at the studio," your mind creates a picture of you leaving the yoga mat at the studio. Instead, you need to say, "I want to remember to bring my yoga mat home with me."

After my husband had come home from work and made that statement, he suddenly became clear about what kind of work he wanted to do. He said, "I would really rather work in the repair shop, and I'd rather work from 8 a.m. to 5 p.m., instead of 9 a.m. to 6 p.m.

At a mandatory work meeting he had to attend two days later, the service manager's assistant didn't show up, and the general manager was upset about it. My husband was offered his job—a promotion—where he would now work 8 a.m. to 5 p.m. and no longer have to drive around and sit alone in traffic all day.

A friend of mine started dating a guy and she was really starting to like him after about three dates. When he didn't respond to a text message she had sent to him one night, she became upset and started to assume that he was purposefully ignoring the text. So she deleted his phone number from her cell phone.

I thought this was a bit reactive and I asked her if in any other situation, she would completely disregard someone just because they didn't answer a text. I said, "What if he didn't get it? Or what if he did respond but the text just didn't make it to you? If I hadn't responded to one of your texts, you would have just asked me, 'Did you get my text?' So why treat this person any differently?"

My friend became frustrated and said, "Well, what am I supposed to do? Just put myself out there and be vulnerable?"

Well, yes. What direction do you want to look in? Do you want to "not be vulnerable"? Or do you want to find love? Because you cannot find love without being vulnerable, and if not being vulnerable is your priority, don't even bother looking for love.

March 2021

Over a decade later, Mark referred to us as "Two peas in a pod, a match made in hell" after he learned I had been in a psychiatric unit trying to cut myself with a sharpened plastic butter knife, right before we met each other.

Mark and I have since healed from our pasts and are very good friends today. He is a good man and has an amazing relationship with his daughter. The kind of relationship every mother hopes her daughter will have with her father. And I have so much respect and love for him for that. Mark has always been so apologetic about those weeks he spent at my house. How he feels terrible for putting me through everything. For bringing his suicide attempt into my life. For repeating the trauma of my mother.

But I never needed him to apologize to me for that. It meant the world to me that he had trusted me during his darkest hour. I was never upset with him for coming to me. I wanted to be there for him and wish I could have done more.

It is incredible to me, how like attracts like. I mean, the

laws of attraction really do work, though not always the way you want them to. So you must be mindful to speak and think in positives. We were on the same track. Just like my college therapist said.

Whether on a motorcycle or in life, you have got to always look in the direction that you want to go. Of course, there are often forks in the road, and a change of course might be needed. The roads I took were rarely the easy ones, yet they often led me to exactly where I needed to be.

8

ZEN MOTORCYCLE HABIT #8

PRACTICE MINDFULNESS, FOCUSING ON WHAT YOU'RE DOING, WHEN YOU'RE DOING IT, AND IN THE CORRECT ORDER

"When you're depressed, you're living in the past. When you're anxious, you're living in the future. When you're at peace, you're living in the present."

—Lao Tzu, Chinese philosopher

How I trudged through jobs and relationships mindlessly for years

Sometimes, it's hard to live in the present. Especially when the present moment sucks.

As a child, the present was not a place I wanted to live in. I felt like I was putting everything on hold, waiting for my mother's mind to return. Hoping someday her manic depression and schizophrenia would just go away. When that day came, then I could finally be happy.

As I became an adult, I would find myself looking to the future hoping to save myself from my present. I'd think, "I'll be happy when I graduate from college. When I get a decent paying job. When I move out of my parents' house. When I find my soulmate. When I make more money. When I buy a house. When I marry my soulmate. When I have kids. When the kids can go to the bathroom by themselves. When the kids go off to college. When I get my kitchen remodeled. When I get a divorce. When I retire."

I treated my life like it was a series of to-do lists. A human-doing instead of a human-being, only when I had checked off every single thing on my list could I finally allow myself to relax and be happy. Then I worried about growing old too fast and not having enough time to "be happy." As if "being happy" is a destination. What I needed was to learn to love the process of life. Was I even enjoying the process of pursuing my goals? I don't know if I ever asked myself that.

Winter 2007

After Mark and I stopped seeing each other, I fell back into a deep depression. I didn't want to deal with how I was feeling. I didn't want to focus on the present.

I needed a new fix. And I found one. Darren.

Darren lived in Oregon. I was in California. We met online. Tattooed, with shaggy blonde ringlets of hair, he was a social worker for at-risk kids that were living in the inner city. He also ran a pit-bull rescue and lived at a sanctuary up in the forest. He played the drums, considered himself a liberal femi-nist, read books about social justice, loved quirky independent films, and meditated on the weekends at a Zen Buddhist Monastery.

Hello? Was this guy for real? I couldn't have invented someone more perfect for myself if I tried. I needed an escape from my shitty life. And I thought Darren was the answer. But timing is everything. It wasn't the right time for us.

Not being mindful when I started that relationship, I was in denial about how bad off I was in my own life. Also, I wasn't doing things in the correct order. Getting ahead of myself, I didn't give myself the time and room to heal from my last two relationships. I couldn't bear the thought of being alone, so I was impulsively trying to out-run my pain. I still hadn't figured out how to save myself. Bottom line: I wasn't ready for a new relationship. And because of that, I ended up hurting Darren.

Still struggling with an identity crisis since my band broke up, I had no clue what I was going to do for a living. I'd thought of myself as a singer for the last three decades, and now was struggling to figure out what to do for money. The best option seemed to be to leave Los Angeles and go to Portland, Oregon to give my relationship with Darren a shot. Maybe the rain wouldn't be as bad as everyone says it is up there. On a positive note, Oregon hospitals hadn't outsourced their medical transcription jobs to Pakistan yet, so maybe I could go back to my old career. I could still see my friends from Los Angeles once a year at the Burning Man festival.

Portland, Oregon is a very nice city to visit. Locals love to show off their beautiful city to out-of-towners. But if the locals get wind that you are a transplant from Los Angeles, look out! Oregonians don't like Angelenos and aren't shy about it. People from Los Angeles come there and drive up the prices, I'm told.

Everything in Oregon was about one-third the price of Los Angeles. But it's really difficult to get a full-time job there. And they pay about a third less than what you'd make in California. Companies will hire on a temporary basis, three months at a time. If they don't like you after three months, then it's sayonara, bitches.

I moved in with Darren so fast, my friends got whiplash. Darren had a nice house and a large piece of property about fifty miles outside of Portland. He ran his pit-bull sanctuary there. When he was at work, I felt extremely isolated and lonely.

He didn't have a TV antenna, satellite, cable, or internet connection. A century ago, the town Darren lived in had a population of 1,100 people. And now, one hundred years later, the population had only increased to 1,800. There was very little infrastructure up there. The water pressure would sometimes run out in the middle of a shower. I'd have to go outside and reset the pump in a bathrobe with shampoo in my eyes.

Phoebe, my pit bull, and I were living at the pit-bull sanctuary with Darren. In the afternoon while Darren was at work, I'd let the pit bulls out in the yard for exercise and potty breaks. He had this one big pit bull who was deaf. When he tried to bark, he sounded like an old man whining with peanut butter stuck in his throat. I was trying to call the dogs back into the house, but the deaf one couldn't hear me. He kept attacking a rope that was hanging from a branch and swinging from it. I was jumping up and down waving my arms like an idiot. I finally started flashing the outdoor light on and off and he came running into the house, knocking me over onto the wet grass. It rained in Oregon. A lot. I didn't realize how much I would miss the sun.

The imposter syndrome I was experiencing was huge, because I couldn't keep a job up there, either. I'd been warned that Portland is a difficult place to find work and keep work. I had contacted an employment agency before I left Los Angeles and hit it off pretty well with my agent, a bubbly young redhead who was due to give birth in about seven weeks. She helped me secure a temporary job in a hospital as a medical transcriber. Unfortunately, the commute was about an hour and a half drive from Darren's house. I would wake up at 4:30 a.m. and leave for work at 5:30 a.m. to get there by 7 a.m. Then I wouldn't get home until 7:30 p.m.

Because my commute was so long, I'd shown up late for work one time too many, and they didn't renew my contract after my three months was up. Admittedly, I wasn't all that upset about not keeping that job. The hours and the commute were long, and the work was boring as hell.

My agent then found another job for me, this time at a chiropractor's office. Just another tedious job full of mindless paperwork and answering phones. I struggled to keep my eyes open when working the front desk, while Enya and other homogenous new age tunes played in the background. One day, I walked into the chiropractor's office to hand him a patient's chart. There was hardcore porn up on his screen. I bolted out of the office, but it was really awkward from then on. His assistant asked me why I always looked so uncomfortable and miserable. I was happy when that assignment ended, too.

Not wanting to deal with long commutes from the wilderness anymore, I started to look for a place to live closer to the city. Plus, I didn't like living so far away from downtown where all the action, music, cafés, and bars were. Darren was sad that I didn't want to stay at the pit-bull sanctuary anymore, but I needed to start creating a life of my own if I was going to stay in Portland. I ended up renting a room in a house in southwest Portland with Suzie and Christopher, my two awesome new roommates. They let me bring Phoebe over sometimes, too. We went out for margaritas and tacos the day I moved in, and Suzie ad Christopher introduced me to their friends. We watched documentaries in the basement living room together while drinking beer and eating pizza. Everything they did should have made me feel at home. Instead, I felt ungrounded, like I was in a strange place where I didn't belong.

My third job was a short train ride from my new place. A beautiful old Victorian house on the northwest side of town that had been turned into an office building, was now home to a large private practice of psychiatrists. I was entering billing data into a computer, as well as faxing medication orders to the pharmacy for about ten different psychiatrists.

"Hmm, I've been on that medication cocktail before," I'd

find myself thinking, quite often, when looking at the prescriptions before feeding them into the fax machine.

The office manager was a nice Asian-American lady in her thirties, about the same age as me. She was an excellent boss, very patient and kind. I could tell she really liked me, and I wasn't surprised when she offered me a full-time position. However, I had to turn it down. I'd come to realize that Portland just wasn't my home, and I didn't want a career as a medical secretary.

I was feeling remorseful. None of my decisions that led me to Oregon had been mindful. They had been impulsive. I was getting ahead of myself and hadn't been doing things in the correct order. I was also feeling awful about impulsively marrying Tiago, then leaving town. Especially after I told him I'd stay married to him so he could get his green card, even though we broke up. He was really upset that I'd moved to Oregon, because he was going to have to meet with immigration soon and prove that our marriage had been real. He needed me to be there, and I was letting him down.

On top of all that, I was feeling awful about Mark. I missed him so much and found myself comparing everyone else I dated to him. I hated myself for that, while simultaneously hating myself for not being stronger for him. I was too needy, insecure, and emotionally battered at the time I met him to be a good friend to him. Then I came to Portland to run away from everything in Los Angeles that was hurting me.

But you know how the old saying goes, "Wherever you go, there you are."

JoAnna from the dispensary in West Hollywood would sometimes text me, "If you ever want your job back, it's waiting for you." Even though my colleagues at the dispensary helped me get off venlafaxine, and I was so grateful for that, I feared the stigma associated with working at a cannabis dispensary. It might inhibit my ability to obtain other jobs in the future. I stayed in Oregon for nine months after going through three temporary jobs. Then, in September, my green card husband, Tiago, got a letter from the Department of Homeland Security. We had an appointment for an interview with Immigration in December. He asked me to move back to Los Angeles. Not to get back together, he was clear, but to finish what we started. He needed his green card. I wanted to keep my word.

He wired me $2,000 to use to move back to Los Angeles and find a place to live. He also said I could use the money for some car repairs I needed. My decade-old Honda needed to survive the one-thousand-mile drive back to Los Angeles. I lied to myself, saying I would only stay in Los Angeles until we were done with Immigration.

I left Phoebe with Darren, again trying to convince myself I'd be back. But even he knew I was lying to myself. I even kept paying rent to Suzie and Christopher for a month or two after I'd left. But I already knew deep down, Oregon was not my home. Latching onto Darren's life made me realize I needed to be living my own life. I needed to start doing things in the right order, and I needed to start making more mindful decisions with my life.

I needed to address my misdiagnoses and take care of my mental and physical health. I needed to end my green card marriage officially and completely before I could think about a new relationship. It was time to decide what I "wanted to be when I grew up."

The day I left Portland for California was a disaster. I accidentally locked Phoebe in the basement and couldn't get ahold of either of my roommates to get her out. Darren and I watched Phoebe from outside the basement window, pacing and nervous. I completely broke down and started freaking out, yelling, screaming, and crying.

"I can't take it anymore!" I wailed. Everything in my life had become so difficult. I felt like I couldn't do the simplest tasks without fucking them up. Poor Phoebe. I felt like I couldn't even take care of my dog properly.

Eventually, I got in touch with Christopher, and he ran home on his lunch break to unlock the basement door and let Phoebe out.

The last thing I remember is getting in my car and wailing like a toddler. Darren stood there holding Phoebe in his arms and was trying not to cry.

And I fucking hated myself.

The drive from Portland to Los Angeles is always longer that I expect it to be. I was crossing over the mountains that separate Oregon from California when I saw the sign that said, "Welcome to California" and spontaneously broke into tears of joy.

As promised, JoAnna offered me my job back at the dispensary when she found out I was in town. I told her I wasn't sure if I was going to stay in Los Angeles. She told me I could start working there again anyway, if I wanted to. Even if it was just temporary. I realized I needed to stay, though. Pretty much as soon as I exited the 405 freeway into Manhattan Beach, I knew I wasn't going back to Oregon. I had too many loose ends to tie up. I had promises to keep. I had some healing to do. Some bridges to mend.

Rents in Los Angeles had skyrocketed during the months I'd been away in Oregon. I couldn't find an affordable place with a yard in a good neighborhood that would let me keep my dog. I felt bad thinking of making Phoebe live in a place without a grassy yard. She would be stuck inside a studio apartment in the city with me all the time. So I made a difficult decision and asked Darren to officially adopt Phoebe from me.

"I can't look at her without thinking of you," Darren said.

"I don't have a good place for her. I don't want to take her away from you and the other dogs. As soon as I find a place to live, I'll bring her here. She's still my dog!" I know I sounded bitchy when I was asking this, but I was at my wit's end.

Unfortunately, I never found a place for Phoebe with me that was better than with Darren. He did end up adopting her permanently and she became his therapy dog until the day she died fifteen years later. I knew I couldn't give her what he could. I felt like a complete failure, but at least I'd gotten Phoebe into the best home ever.

November 2007

Back in Los Angeles, I initially thought I was going to stay in the guest room in the back of the house Tiago and some other guys from Brazil were renting. When I made it to Tiago's place and tried to hug him, he looked at me and coldly stated, "You can't just come back here like this and expect me to love you." Feeling dejected, I called my good friend Danielle, who was renting a place in Glassell Park on the Eastside of Los Angeles. "Why don't you just stay with me tonight. It's got to be really uncomfortable trying to live with your ex," she offered.

I had not even unpacked my stuff at Tiago's and was already back in my car heading to the opposite end of Los Angeles to Danielle's place. About forty minutes into my drive, and ten minutes from Danielle's apartment, my phone suddenly rang. Holy shit. Mark was calling me. We hadn't spoken in a year. My stomach started buzzing as soon as I saw his name. Clearly, I still had a thing for him.

When I answered, he asked, "Hey cool breeze, how is it up there in Portland?" He was back at Schwarzenegger's bar having a beverage, and it had made him think of me, since we used to frequent the place, he explained.

"I literally just moved back to L.A., like, a few hours ago."

"Oh wow!" He sounded happily surprised. "I didn't know

you'd been planning to move back. Where are you? Want to meet me at Schwarzenegger's?"

I hadn't even been back in town for three hours. The drive from Portland to Los Angeles took me over seventeen hours. I hadn't slept in nearly twenty-four hours and was now heading back to a bar forty minutes away on the Westside of Los Angeles.

Mark looked as good as I remembered when I saw him sitting there on that bar stool, even dressed down in a white T-shirt and faded jeans. He greeted me with a hug.

After ordering a couple of whiskey and cokes, and catching up on small talk, Mark said, "I've been really wanting to talk to you about everything that happened last summer. My suicide attempt really messed up my sister. She was pretty devastated when she found out. A lot of my friends had a really hard time with it. But I think I really messed you up more than all of them, and I've been feeling terrible about it."

I really needed this conversation. Like, reeeeally needed to have this talk. But I wanted to get a fix from Mark more than I wanted to have this conversation. Mark didn't know the half of it. He didn't know the full history of my mother's mental illness, or her suicide attempts. He didn't know the depth of my codependency or my abandonment issues. He wasn't privy to all my psychiatric diagnoses or the various pharmaceuticals I'd been on. It was too much to get into.

Not wanting him to think that my mental instability had anything to do with his actions, I made light of the situation. I downplayed how much it had affected me to the core. I didn't want to admit how badly I'd fallen for him that summer. How much he broke my heart into pieces, and how I was comparing everyone else to him. I didn't want him to feel the need to shoulder my own pain on top of his. Bottom line, I didn't want to be a burden to him.

"I was totally fucked up before you met me, Mark. It's not your fault. I'm a hot mess. I was messed up long before you came into the picture." I laughed nervously. I could tell he wasn't buying it by the concerned look on his face.

I couldn't deal with the emotions that were starting to come up. I needed to switch the subject. Fast.

"Hey, why don't we go and have sex for old time's sake?"

Mark paused. There was a look of hesitation in his eyes. He might have even said, "I don't know if that's a good idea…"

He sighed heavily, as if to acknowledge how emotionally unhealthy my suggestion was. But it didn't stop us. I quickly texted Danielle that I wasn't going to be crashing at her place tonight after all. Barely back in Los Angeles for three hours, and I was naked in bed with Mark.

Of course, the next day, I felt absolutely horrible about myself. I knew I was going back to my job at the dispensary working with medical marijuana patients, and I couldn't be with Mark and risk putting custody over his daughter in jeopardy. I was broke and this was the only job offering me a living wage that I was qualified for. I'd play the conversation over and over in my head. I'd confess my true feelings for him, that I wanted to be with him and no one else. But it always ended up the same way, with us not being together because I was worried about his daughter. Why bother even having such a painful conversation when things were just going to end the same way, whether he returned my feelings or not?

So, once again, I kept my mouth shut.

December 2007

Two months after uncomfortably settling back into Los Angeles at Tiago's Brazilian bachelor pad, we attended our interview, or rather, interrogation at the Department of Homeland Security. We had a box full of love letters, gifts, photo albums, greeting cards, and statements from our joint bank account. Everything we needed to prove our relationship had been real. It really had been real. People in fake relationships do not bicker the way Tiago and I did.

We were the only people at the immigration office that morning, and it made us nervous. We were interrogated for an hour by an immigration officer. He said our marriage didn't make sense, because I was ten years older than him. Plus, we had only known each other for two months when we got married.

I started revealing things to the immigration officer that I was discovering about myself in real time. Yes, we had gotten married after only two months. I was in an emotional crisis at the time. I had been taking an antidepressant that made me impulsive. I had not been mindful when I was making my decision to get married. But our relationship had been real.

"So," the immigration officer asked, "do you think if you hadn't been on the wrong psychiatric medications, you would have still married him?"

"No. I probably wouldn't have."

Tiago looked embarrassed.

"Okay, then. Thank you for being honest." Then he said to me, "I'm going to let you make the decision. Do you think he deserves to stay in the United States? I will say, he's probably going to leave you as soon as he gets that green card."

"I'm the one who already failed the relationship," I confessed. "He deserves the green card. He is a good person."

"Okay, then," the officer stated.

Suddenly, his tone changed from "bad cop" to "good cop."

"You know, I'm really sorry for grilling you like that. I'm not really sure why they made you come down in person," he said. "I saw all the cards and letters and photos you submitted. It's obvious this was a real relationship, even if it didn't work out in the end. I've seen green cards get approved on much less."

Then he turned to Tiago and said, "Welcome to the United States."

What a relief. We could finally put this behind us. In the elevator on the way out, Tiago and I embraced each other and cried tears of relief. He asked me how I felt about my country after that experience.

"I'm a little annoyed. I don't know why they needed to interrogate us like that. We had submitted all the paperwork and proof that we'd had a real relationship."

"You know what I think?" Tiago asked me. "What I saw was one American trying to protect another American. That is a great deal of power your country gave you. You got to decide whether I was allowed to stay in this country legally. I saw one American making sure another fellow American wasn't taken advantage of by a foreigner."

I thought that was an enlightened way of looking at the situation.

Tiago stayed in Los Angeles after that. He's still in Los Angeles to this day. He went on to get married a few years later. He has two adorable children with his REAL wife.

Meanwhile, I spent the next few years mending my life in Los Angeles. It was a difficult process. It wasn't the last time I had gotten ahead of myself, though. But I can say it was the beginning of my long journey towards healing.

It was only the start of understanding the importance of living a mindful life.

January 2008

I received a disturbing call from my father one afternoon when I was hanging out with some girlfriends.

"Les. Have you heard from your mom recently? The bank called me and said she hasn't cashed any of my alimony checks in a year."

Wait. Had it really been a year since the last time I spoke

to my mother? I tried to remember if we'd ever spoken while I was living in Portland. My mother would go missing from time to time. The usual pattern of hers was that she would feel great on a medication protocol, think she was cured, and stop taking her meds. It would take a few weeks for the meds to wear off and for her behavior to get funky. She'd then end up in the hospital for a month or two, and then I'd hear from her maybe four to six months later once she had "cleared up." The longest I'd gone without hearing from her was usually three to six months. Never this long. Not a whole year.

Panic-stricken, I called up all the usual relatives on my mom's side of the family: her sister, her brother, her mother, her aunt. No one had been in contact with my mother in about a year. Her sister, my Aunt Claudia, told me that my mother may have gone off her medication yet again. Last she had heard, my mother was fighting with her landlord, and my Aunt Claudia had wondered if my mom had been illegally evicted. I called the police department in Fayetteville, Arkansas and gave them my mother's address so they could do a welfare check on her. Several days later, the police department informed me she had moved out of that apartment six months ago, per her landlord.

My mother was missing.

The more time ticked on without hearing from my mom, the darker I felt inside. What kind of a daughter loses track of her mother? I imagined her wrapped up in a blanket in some dark, dirty alleyway, dead from hypothermia. A once bright and beautiful pixie-ballerina, discarded like a piece of trash, with a piece of shit daughter who did nothing to save her.

I was powerless, and thoughts of my mother haunted me.

Unable to find an affordable apartment on my dispensary salary, I'd been staying in a bedroom in the house where my ex, Tiago, and his friends from Brazil were living. After a few very awkward weeks, Danielle said her offer still stood and I could couch surf at her new apartment.

We made it official when we turned the garage under her one-bedroom apartment into a little studio for me. I paid her $350 a month in rent, but rarely slept down there. We became convinced that the apartment, and the garage in particular, were haunted. A dirty outline of a large cross stained one of the walls in the basement and we could not scrub it off. It gave us both the chills. So Danielle said she understood if I wanted to sleep on the couch upstairs.

Every night it seemed one, if not both, of us were having terrifying sleep paralysis dreams, those dreams that happen when your mind is awake but your body is still asleep and you can't move. There are many cultures with some version of this sleep-demon. It is most commonly known as "The Hag." Whenever "The Hag" would visit us in our sleep, Danielle would try to rationalize it. "I used to have night terrors all the time in college when I was stressed out."

"Yes, but we are both having the same exact nightmares, which is kind of freaking me out," I pointed out. We both kept having the same vivid dream about a Filipino or Hispanic woman named Alma shuffling around our apartment wearing light-blue slippers and a robe.

One night, Danielle was having trouble falling asleep. Right before we went to bed, we had watched something on the news about Heath Ledger's accidental overdose which had led to his death. Between that and the hauntings we were experiencing, we were both suffering from many sleepless nights. There were some cannabis-infused iced-tea drinks in our fridge that I'd brought home from work. They worked really well for me when I was having insomnia, so I recommended that Danielle try one before bedtime.

Well, I totally forgot that Danielle is a lightweight when it comes to cannabis, and she woke up in the middle of the night having a really bad trip.

"Leslie? Are you awake?" I woke up to Danielle standing over the living room couch that I was sleeping on, because I was too creeped out that night to sleep in the garage-turned-bedroom downstairs.

"What's the matter? Is everything okay?"

"Ummm…." she said nervously, looking like she was about to cry, "I think…that cannabis iced tea?"

"Yeah, what about it?"

"Are you sure there wasn't anything else in it? Because I feel like I'm going to die."

Then she burst into full-blown tears and cried, "I'm going to die just like Heath Ledger!"

I couldn't help myself and started laughing.

"No, there's nothing else in that drink. OMG, I'm so sorry. It must have been too strong for you, and it made you really paranoid."

"Are you sure?" She continued to cry like a kindergartener whose favorite teddy bear has been stolen. "Are you sure I'm not going to die like Heath Ledger?"

"Yes, I'm positive. You cannot die from a cannabis iced-tea. I promise. You're just freaking out because this apartment is probably haunted. Come on, sweetie, let me help you back to bed."

Danielle continued wailing. I walked her to the foot of her bed, and she fell face down flat onto the mattress, with her legs dangling straight out from the foot of the bed.

"Okay, you need to crawl yourself up to the pillows. Your legs are, like, totally hanging out of the bed," I said as I tried in vain to push the bottom of Danielle's feet with the palms of my hands to get her all the way up to the head of her bed.

"I can't! I can't!" She continued to cry face down in a voice muffled by her mattress, "I'm going to die like Heath Ledger!"

"Girl, you are going to have to help me out here."

Whimpering the entire time, Danielle was finally able to crawl herself all the way into bed. She cried herself to sleep, but alas, she did not die like Heath Ledger.

Then there was this other freaky haunted incident where I'd gone over to Mark's place and stayed overnight. Danielle had been hired to DJ at a club that night and wasn't home when I left.

The next morning, I got back to our apartment just as the sun was coming up. Danielle's face was pale. "Did you just get home?" she asked.

"Yeah, why? Are you okay?"

"I thought I heard you come home really early, at like two or three o'clock this morning and I started having a conversation with you. I could have sworn you answered me when I asked you if you'd bolted the front door. I heard footsteps shuffling down the hall. Seriously? You're just getting home now? I thought you were home this whole time."

Danielle and I agree to this day that apartment was the creepiest, most haunted place either of us had ever lived in. We were never fully able to admit how scary and real that haunting felt until we both finally moved out of that place.

The scariest experience I had at that place happened one morning as I lay frozen in bed by sleep paralysis in the creepy garage turned bedroom. A figure of my mother, her face distraught with anger, hovered over me. Her hands were on my shoulders, and she was shaking me while holding me down onto the bed. I woke up to the sound of my own voice saying, "Mom. You're scaring me." Just then, I noticed my coworker "Dr. Phill" from the dispensary sitting on the edge of my bed saying, "I told you, if your house is haunted, you need to burn sage and get the smoke into the corners!" I woke up from that dream within a dream in a cold sweat.

Believing that my mother's spirit had visited me that morning, I was sure it meant she was dead. I was devastated. She was angry with me. She looked like she had wanted to kill me. Who could blame her? The California sun could no longer penetrate the darkness that had overtaken me. The blue sky only served to mock me. I had never been able to get my shit together enough the way I wanted to so I could take care of her. I wanted to be a famous singer so I could pay for the best psychiatric care on the planet. I had failed myself and failed my mother. And now she was probably dead.

March 2008

Mark would continue to call me sporadically, usually from a bar, and would ask me if I wanted to meet up for a drink. He never asked me on dates anymore. Desperate for validation, I had a difficult time saying no to him.

When we would get together, we would always avoid talking about the incident when he almost took his own life the summer before. If it did come up, we would casually gloss over it and minimize it, never really addressing what it had done to either one of us, emotionally. Usually, we'd avoid the whole topic altogether by going off somewhere to have sex. Afterwards, I'd always feel like pure shit because I knew a real relationship with him would be impossible. The quiet calm I used to feel with him before the "incident" was long gone. I had been triggered back into my fight or flight responses and would freeze like a deer in headlights as soon as I'd try to address any real emotions I had with Mark.

Sometimes when he would call, I'd have the willpower to say no. Other times, I found myself missing him so bad, I just couldn't resist, and I'd give in.

Like the time I was on my way to see my roommate, Danielle, DJ at a warehouse party downtown. Mark had texted me when I was on my way. He was with Randy and some other friends of his. They were looking for something fun to do on a Friday night, so I said he and his friends could meet me at the warehouse party. As soon as I saw him with his friends waiting for me in front of the warehouse, I knew it was a mistake.

I suddenly realized I'd gravely misjudged that seeing Mark

tonight had been a good idea. I still needed to process the effect his suicide attempt had had on me. I needed to address my conflicting feelings about wanting to be in a relationship with him, while fully understanding why there were too many real reasons why that couldn't happen.

Not only that, I barely processed the fact that my mother had gone missing, and now I was triggered.

Like the full moon that night causing the ocean's tides to swell, my panic swelled out of control within me, and awkwardness took over.

My anxiety was so loud, I could barely hear the music pounding around me over the beating of my heart. As the inside of the warehouse became a red blur around us, Mark pulled me onto the dance floor with him, but he could see I was distracted.

"Come outside with me while I have a cigarette," he said.

We sat on the bench in front of the club, and he pulled me onto his lap.

"I'm sorry I'm acting so weird," I told him, feeling like I was on the verge of breaking into tears. "I don't know what's wrong with me."

I did know what was wrong with me but couldn't find a way to put it into words.

What was wrong was that I had blown off the conversation the one time Mark tried to have a serious discussion with me. I wasn't prepared to have that conversation right after I moved back from Portland, but it was an important conversation that really needed to happen.

I needed to talk to him about all the unanswered questions I had, and how "the incident" had affected me more than I realized, or even wanted to admit. I needed to explain why I was no longer acting like the same carefree girl he had met two summers ago. I needed to unburden myself of the triggers from my past. I needed him to know that I had some painful old wounds that were re-opening because I recently found out my schizophrenic mother had gone missing, and that much of my awkward behavior was really about that. I wanted to tell him how I was struggling to differentiate my emotions that belonged to him and the ones that were just echoes of my own past trauma.

Instead, I just froze.

After lighting his cigarette, he pulled me closer onto his lap and said, "So many people love you, Leslie. And I'm one of them…"

Just then, before he had a chance to finish what he was saying, we noticed his friends Randy and Shanita stumbling out of the warehouse and walking towards Randy's car together.

"Hold on a minute." Mark slid me off his lap onto the bench and ran after his two friends. I couldn't make out what any of them were saying.

"I've got to go. I have to make sure my friend Shanita is safe getting in a car with Randy," he said in a hurry, grabbing his jacket off the bench.

"Wait, what?"

"I'm so sorry, I just need to make sure she is alright," he said.

"After you make sure she's alright, are you coming back?" I pleaded, as I wasn't done with this conversation, and it had barely gotten started.

"It's already kind of late…" He said, practically running away from me.

So I pulled out the "sex" card.

"Are you sure you don't want to come over tonight?"

"No, I better not. I have a lot of stuff to do in the morning."

His two friends were already in the car. Mark yelled at them to wait and ran to his truck. He made an illegal U-turn and was on their tail. I watched him screech out of sight.

Paralyzed with anxiety, and having no idea what the fuck

just happened, I sat alone on the bench downtown trying to catch my breath. I was uncomfortably close to Skid Row. A homeless man walked by with a shopping cart full of dirty blankets and water bottles, neither of us acknowledging the other. I couldn't bring myself to get up, and my ears were ringing.

Danielle's voice cut through the din that was clouding my mind and asked, "What happened? Why are you sitting out here all alone? It's dangerous to be out here by yourself. Where did Mark go?"

"I don't know. I was sitting here with Mark. He told me that so many people love me, and that he was one of them. Then before he could finish his sentence, he said he had to make sure his friends were safe or something, and he went after them. I'm so confused."

"What? Do you think maybe he likes Shanita and was upset she left with Randy? Or maybe he is just worried they are too drunk to drive?"

"Yeah, but then I asked him if he wanted to come over after he made sure Shanita was safe, and then he said he had too much stuff to do in the morning. But tomorrow is Saturday, so I don't know…"

Seeing the distraught look on my face, Danielle tried to console me. "Aww, I'm so sorry. It sounds like he was about to tell you he loved you, just, you know. Not that way. I think you may have just gotten friend-zoned. But, hey, it's good to know he loves you as a friend, right?" Danielle said compassionately.

"Yeah, maybe not," she added, seeing my blank stare.

Friend-zoned. That seemed like an accurate observation to me, and once again, I found myself listening to "Protection" by Massive Attack on repeat while eating Haagen-Dazs double chocolate chip ice cream on the couch.

I told myself I wasn't going to meet up with him at the last minute at bars anymore. No more midnight bootie calls, and no more spontaneous meet-ups for drinks. There was no turning back to what we had before "the incident." I needed to cut the cord. I was only hurting myself.

But, when Mark texted me on a Monday a couple weeks later and asked if I wanted to go see *Slumdog Millionaire* with him that Friday, a flicker of hope lit up inside me. We were making a plan for a date in advance. I thought to myself, "Finally. Maybe after the movie, I can have a down-to-earth talk with Mark about how I really feel. Maybe I can find that quiet place with him again. Even if we are just going to be friends. Not at a bar, a warehouse party, or high at a club, we can finally have that talk."

After rearranging my schedule at the dispensary to make sure I was off work on Friday night for our first real date since the incident, I texted Mark to find out where we were meeting and when.

"Oh shit! I totally forgot! Went to Vegas with some friends last minute!" his text read. "Sorry!" A second text read.

The hope within me deflated like a balloon. And then it got worse.

Pouring salt into my wounds, when I logged onto Facebook the following Monday, Mark's "friend," a pretty blond from the Midwest, had tagged him in multiple photos from their last-minute trip to Las Vegas. Holding up big frozen oversized alcoholic beverages adorned with paper umbrellas and cherries, the two of them smiled, intoxicated, striking various corny poses for the camera while leaning into each other. The backdrops varied from ostentatious casino entryways to colorful slot machines.

While my stomach bottomed out every photo I scrolled past in my feed of the two of them, Facebook alerted me that Mark was online. Then it alerted me that Mark had tagged me in a photo. Clicking the alert, I found myself looking at a picture of myself with Mark. Mark had changed his main profile picture to a selfie he had taken of the two of us from two years ago. The night we had danced all night in a room full of pink and red glitter and fairies. Was this his way of apologizing? A third alert informed me that Mark had sent me a message.

"I'm really sorry I forgot about Friday," he wrote. "That girl I'm in the pictures with is an old friend of mine from my hometown. She was going through a rough time and needed a friend."

My already-frozen heart shattered like un-tempered glass.

What about my "rough times"? Did it ever occur to Mark that I might need a friend?

Never wanting to burden him with my own problems, he probably had no idea how bad my "rough times" were, or how much my soul was rotting away inside. I always tried to put up a solid front for him.

Knowing my mother was missing had put me in the darkest place imaginable, and I desperately could have used a last-minute trip to Vegas with him. Or anywhere for that matter. Yet Mark seemed like he was concerned about every other woman's well-being but mine. Chasing after his friend Shanita to make sure she was safe, but then leaving me alone on a bench downtown. Forgetting he said he wanted to go to the movies with me, then ditching me for yet another damsel in distress in Vegas.

Not wanting to feel like his plan B anymore, and tired of allowing myself to get my heart broken by him repeatedly, I sent him a message back, telling him I was confused by his behavior and needed to step away. "I can't be your friend right now," I messaged him. Then I "unfriended" him and called Danielle.

"Leslie," she said with all the usual compassion in her voice, "maybe you need to really just tell Mark how you feel about him? Like, just be straight? Does he have any idea what you are going through with your mother missing? You guys have never really talked since you moved back to Los Angeles.

He probably has no idea how much you are hurting or how much you care about him."

"How can he not know?" I sobbed, feeling like the biggest loser on the planet. "I just don't think it's worth it, Danielle. I feel like he's just kicking it with me until someone better comes along. Like, where did my self-respect go? It's like I keep standing in front of a moving train and wondering why I keep getting hurt.

"And even if he did have feelings for me," I continued, "I know he has to focus on his daughter. He's still living with his sister. He couldn't give me what I need even if he wanted to. I'm pretty sure he doesn't love me anyway."

"Well," Danielle sighed, "I still think you should tell him how you really feel. You can't be sure he knows exactly what you are going through unless you tell him."

She was right. I needed to speak my truth. Trying to ignore the way I was feeling was just making things worse. Mark wasn't a mind reader. But the gaping hole in my chest couldn't bear any more disappointment. Believing Mark needed a woman who had her shit together, and not someone working at a weed dispensary one paycheck away from living in the gutter, I didn't see the point. Whoever Mark needed, I believed that wasn't me. So, again, I kept my mouth shut.

The real reason I didn't say anything, though, was because I was afraid of what the truth might be. Maybe he just didn't have feelings for me the way I did for him and the thought of confirming that was more than I could stand. His actions, by my definition, were already telling me loud and clear, "Guuu-url, he's just not that into you." So I just shoved everything I was feeling down as far as it would go.

I wasn't being mindful about my emotions or respecting where I was in my own mental health healing process. I was continuing to run away from the things I needed to address.

Yet, I had no idea how we'd ended up here.

Mark did, however, leave the profile picture of the two of

us up for several weeks. I think it was the only way he knew how to apologize to me.

~

Have you ever driven somewhere in your car and realized that you have no recollection of how you got there? Or you're driving down a street and realize you don't know where you are going? Or you meant to drive to the bank, but instead started driving to the grocery store?

This is the opposite of mindfulness. It's dangerous to do in a car, but even more dangerous to do on a motorcycle.

I wanted to adopt the habit of being mindful to help myself learn to ride a motorcycle. To focus on what I'm doing when I'm doing it, and to do things in the correct order. That's all mindfulness is: paying attention to what you're doing, when you're doing it.

Sounds so simple, right? Yet how many of us do this?

Driving is one of those things that becomes automatic after many years of having a license. We sometimes stop being mindful when we are doing it. When you're driving, are you creating a laundry list in your head of things you need to do when you get out of the car? Or are you focusing on the traffic? When you're watching television or in a meeting, are you also texting and looking at social media? Or are you focusing 100 percent on what is being said? Are you thinking of things that happened at work earlier in the day? Or are you worrying about the future, and things that haven't happened yet?

So, are you awake at the wheel in your own life?

The Chinese philosopher Lao Tzu once said, "If you're depressed, you're living in the past. If you're anxious, you're living in the future. If you're at peace, you're living in the present."

February 2021

I was having a hard time getting back up on my bike. A few weeks earlier, I dropped my 2021 Zero S electric motorcycle for, like, the third time.

The next time I did get on my bike, I was so nervous I didn't even enjoy myself. That's because I kept thinking about the three times I dropped my motorcycle. And all I could think was, "Whatever you do, don't drop the bike!" As soon as my mind starts to wander on the motorcycle, I start scaring myself. I start thinking about all the mistakes I could make and all the things I could do wrong.

When I stop trusting myself, that's how I know I've stopped being mindful. When I start to panic on the motorcycle, it's because I'm worrying about mistakes I might make in the future, as well as thinking about riding mistakes I've made in the past. I want to learn from my mistakes. Not relive them.

Doing things in the correct order is also part of mindfulness. You cannot learn to ride a motorcycle if you haven't learned to ride a bicycle. You can't shift gears on a motorcycle without first releasing the throttle and pulling in the clutch. Taking steps in the correct order is part of being mindful. Maybe we'd like to be further along in our lives, schoolwork, careers, relationships, and so on, but we need to accept where we are and not get ahead of ourselves.

I thought I might have gotten ahead of myself when I bought my first street bike.

My husband, who has been riding for almost forty years, insisted that if I wanted to learn to ride a motorcycle, I should start on a dirt-bike. He felt I should spend a year on the Kawasaki KX-85 I'd bought on Craigslist before investing in a street bike. However, I have no patience. I wanted to skip the dirt-bike and go right to the street bike. I thought that buying a motorcycle with an automatic transmission would help me learn to ride faster.

Yet the electric motorcycle I bought, like every motorcycle, had its own challenges. Even though it had an automatic transmission, I still had to learn to master other skills to be able to ride my Zero S electric street bike. I was looking too far into the future instead of working with what's right in front of me. And now, I'm dealing with the anxiety of worrying about the next time I get on my motorcycle.

But, when I'm being mindful on the motorcycle, my thoughts do not have a chance to scare me. I'm not reminding myself of the three (or more) times I dropped my motorcycle. Impatience and hypervigilance can lead to impulsiveness. Impulsiveness is the opposite of mindfulness.

Growing up with my schizophrenic mother, the present was something I wanted to get away from as soon as possible. I'd dream of the future, but I had no real process or plan for how to get there. So, instead, I'd get ahead of myself and try to escape the present by living in a future I hadn't set the foundation for.

Even with this book. I started sending out my book proposal before I'd finished my manuscript. I was thinking it would take agents months to get back to me. But a big agent got back to me in less than twenty-four hours. He asked for my manuscript. I realized I'd met an opportunity that I was not prepared for.

Making Mindfulness a Habit

If we practice mindfulness and start living in the present, it can help to ease our anxiety about the future. It can also help us to learn from our past mistakes, instead of dwelling on them. It's important for us to find peace with the present moment.

Sometimes "right now" legitimately sucks, so I'm not going to tell you that living in the present is always calm and blissful. Sometimes, it's not appropriate to feel happy and we just have to make peace with our current situation. Even when that current situation blows. We need to learn to be comfortable with being uncomfortable. We also need to know when it is time to ask for help.

There is a big difference between a case of the blues and clinical depression. There is a misconception that people who are depressed just need to be more grateful about what they have. A person with a clinical diagnosis of depression cannot just "snap out of it." Clinical depression is not caused by a lack of gratitude. So, respect your limits and boundaries. Be patient with yourself and your limits. Understand that you might need help. We can't always just "snap out of it" when we are struggling.

Don't fear that you will be in this place forever. All states are temporary. Our lives are always in flux. So, if you need therapy, get therapy. If you need a psychiatrist, get a psychiatrist. Meditate, run, do yoga. Find something to help you stay present.

Ultimately, there is more than one way to find your way out of a mental health crisis. Sometimes, there is a lot of trial and error involved. Everyone's path to serenity is different. Keep trying until you find something that works.

Practice making mindful decisions, and don't give up.

9

ZEN MOTORCYCLE HABIT #9

PRACTICE GOOD HABITS OFTEN AND COMMIT YOURSELF TO THE PROCESS

"Life is what happens when you are busy making other plans."

—ALLEN SAUNDERS, MADE FAMOUS BY JOHN LENNON

How I came to realize the importance of good habits to mental health

Habits. I had a lot of them. Bad ones.

Growing up in a household with mental illness, there was no time to create healthy habits. I had to be on the edge of my seat, ready for anything. I had to be ready for the unexpected all the time. There is no point in planning to set a routine, when it's only going to get disrupted by the latest crisis. Why bother?

And that's what this entire book is about. How those little, insignificant habits end up making up our entire lives.

I never paid much attention to habits. Bad habits can make your life look like an addict's. Even if you aren't taking any drugs or alcohol. Bad habits can really screw up your life. What are your habits with time? Money? Relationships? Are you consistent with your habits or not? Do you take care of your "future self"? Or has your lack of planning ever inconvenienced, or even harmed, your "future self"? I can definitely say, my unconscious impulsive decisions and poor habits have harmed me due to lack of planning and focus in the past.

Zen happens when we are living life in such a mindful way that mindfulness becomes a habit. When we are in the habit of living mindfully, we aren't worrying about the future, or depressed about the past. We are accepting each moment for what it is.

Before learning to ride a motorcycle, my habits were not mindful. When I'd drive in my car, I rushed to the stop signs, then would slam on the brakes. This habit of racing to a stop sign would lead me to needing new tires and new brakes more often than necessary. This created a financial burden and wasted time in repairs.

Something as simple as changing my braking habits in the car saved me time and money in the long run.

It is not rocket science: a motorcycle is going to do exactly what you tell it to do. If you hit the throttle, the bike will take off whether you want it to or not. I'd done it multiple times, and it only took a fraction of an inch of a wrong movement with my hand to end up violently thrown to the ground leaving a trail of burnt rubber behind me.

The motorcycle followed my unintentional command. And the next thing that happened, we were both down.

Habits are like this, too. All it takes is for one miniscule bad habit to get ahold of you, and at some point, it builds on itself. For instance, say you're in the habit of using your debit card to pay for everything. You're not in the habit of keeping track of the balance in your checking account. Let's say you overspend your checking account by only $5 a month. You will most likely get charged a ridiculous $35 overdraft fee. Or you might end up paying a 35 percent interest rate in overdraft protection. That's just $5 that will end up costing you at least $35.

The difference between happiness and misery is clear. Happiness is spending $5 less than you have every month. Misery is spending $5 more than you have every month. Eventually, those $5 will add up in interest and overdraft fees.

This is why it is so important to practice living mindfully and paying attention to the habits we are creating.

Remember, Zen philosophy says, "How a person does any one thing, is how a person does everything."

You may not have even noticed how your bad habits developed. That's because habits are not something that happens overnight. They start slowly and on a small level over a specific amount of time.

My bad habits really became apparent when I started nursing school.

As a child, school was exhausting for me. Not the school-work, but the other stuff. The playground politics, the social cues, where to sit and who to sit with at lunch.

By the time I got home, I had no energy for homework. Unfortunately, my parents were too preoccupied with my mother's schizophrenia to notice. My inability to fit in with the other kids my age was taking a toll on my schoolwork. Since I didn't have the energy to study for tests, I got really good at writing notes in class. I'd try to remember what was being said as it was being said. This was enough to get me a C- in most classes, and A's and B's in the classes I was actually interested in. But I had never really developed decent study habits.

March 2009

Being the daughter of a schizophrenic, the loved one of an addict, and a mental health patient myself taught me more about mental health than anything they could have tried to teach me in nursing school. With all that I had learned, I began to feel it was my calling to become a psychiatric nurse.

Still in Los Angeles and living on my own, I was continuing to struggle to make ends meet. Almost ten years had passed since I first moved here, and I still had not been able to go to nursing school or find a job that paid a living wage. Although I'd been accepted into more than one nursing school, with no savings to help me, there was not enough time or funding to make it happen. I was already working two jobs and scraping by.

It became clear that to go back to school and realize my professional dreams, I'd have to move home to New Jersey and move back in with my father. Then, I wouldn't have to work, and I'd have time to focus on the coursework. Doing so meant putting my ego aside, but it was worth it. I packed up what little stuff I had, shipped it all to my dad's house, and bought a one-way ticket back to New Jersey.

December 2009

The first winter that I spent back in New Jersey, I got a message from a mental health tech at an assisted living home in West Memphis, Arkansas. My mother was living there.

She hadn't died homeless in some alleyway after all.

I dialed the number the next morning and heard my mother's voice for the first time since the end of 2006. We both broke into tears, and then I scolded her for disappearing on me. "I thought you were dead, Mom," I cried.

My mother attempted to tell me what had happened to her. It was hard to put the entire timeline together. She gave it to me in bits and pieces. She said she'd been evicted from her apartment illegally (later, my Aunt Claudia told me that my mother had been throwing all her belongings, including furniture, out of her apartment window). She described without any emotion how she was living on the street for a while, and one night she was assaulted. A man tried to rape her, she said, but somehow, she was the one who had ended up in police custody. My educated guess as a psychiatric nurse, was that she probably had been put on an involuntary psychiatric hold and brought to a crisis stabilization center, which to many psychiatric patients when off their meds, might feel like jail. My mother then reported that at some point, she was living with some nuns. It turns out my mother had been at the Salvation Army Homeless Shelter in Little Rock for a while. The nuns had later gotten her admitted into the assisted living facility in West Memphis, Arkansas.

In the summer of 2010, I saw my mother for the last time. It was terrible. She was embarrassed and humiliated.

I was in Alabama visiting some family, and realized I was only a five-hour drive from the nursing home in West Memphis, Arkansas where she was living. After getting lost several times, I finally found the facility. I'd been waiting in the lobby for quite some time, when one of the techs came out and told me that visiting hours weren't for another forty-five minutes. So I went to a shopping mall about ten minutes away and bought a new hairdryer, then went back to the facility and waited for what seemed like forever. When the mental health tech finally emerged from the door, he said, "Leslie? I'm sorry to keep you waiting. Come this way."

I followed the mental health care tech down a sterile white hallway to my mother's room. When he opened her door, I heard my mother's voice scream, "You're mean!!!" at him. He brushed her off, turned to me, and let out a nervous chuckle. "She hasn't been very happy today," he said as if she were merely a child throwing a tantrum.

As he left the room, I realized why my mother had screamed at him. She sat on the toilet wearing a dirty scrub top. Her hospital scrub-pants with smudges of poop lay on the tiled floor next to her.

"I was trying to get in the shower. My stomach was upset." She broke into anguished tears.

"It's not supposed to be like this." She was bawling her

eyes out. "You're not supposed to see me like this. This is wrong."

My heart sank.

"Mom, come on. Let me help you. Do you want me to help you get in the shower?"

"No. No. I can't do this. You should go."

"It's okay, Mom. I'll wait. We haven't seen each other in a long time. I'm here now and I can wait. Just get in the shower. I can wait," I pleaded.

Tears still streaming from her eyes, she stood up from the toilet, her teeth and fists clenched in frustration and anger, and began pounding an invisible steering wheel in front of her with both fists.

I started to walk towards her, but she put up her hand.

"Please go. I can't do this. I can't have you seeing me like this."

"Are you sure?...Mom…"

"Yes, please. Just go," she cried.

I'd driven over five hours to see her and had spent another two hours waiting. I was mentally and emotionally exhausted.

"Mom, come on." I reached out and hugged her as she stood there, pants-less.

"I think you should just go," she said calmly.

As I slowly walked out of her room, I felt the same type of relief I'd felt when my therapist advised me against reporting Dan after he raped me: Relieved that someone had given me permission to check-out, while also feeling ashamed that I couldn't deal with the reality of it all. It was a wound that I knew I would never, ever heal from.

Numb, I got into my car. I only drove a few feet out of the parking lot before pulling over. My head was reeling. I put both hands on the sides of my head as if to keep it attached to my body, and let out the shrillest, longest, loudest, most terrifying banshee-inspired scream that I didn't even know I was capable of producing. I screamed so loudly it scared me, as it felt like shards of glass were exploding from my lungs and cutting through everything in sight. It was as if a thousand years of pain had manifested in one scream, creating a black hole of sorrow that swallowed up any light it came in contact with. There would be no closure or recovery from this.

Fall 2011

Continuing to struggle with the mindset that I wasn't going to be good enough with math or science to get through nursing school, I was going to have to learn to quiet that negative inner voice that constantly berated me. I was worried I wouldn't be able to handle the smells, the blood, the poop, and other bodily fluids. I kept forgetting the easiest things, like what a normal blood sugar would be. And I was engaged to a diabetic at the time. In other words, I felt like a big fraud.

I was six weeks pregnant when I started nursing school. My anxiety was shooting through the roof. Part of me was ready to use my pregnancy as an excuse to quit. You know me, when things get too hard, I start believing I have no business doing them.

While testing off on how to give someone a proper bed bath on a mannequin, I suddenly began to bleed. I ran to the bathroom when my fellow classmate, Marilyn, pointed out the blood running down my leg.

Continuing to bleed as I sat on the toilet, I heard someone enter the bathroom.

"Hey, are you okay? It's Marilyn, your classmate."

"Um, I think I'm having a miscarriage."

"Are you still bleeding?"

"Like, a lot."

"Hey, don't freak out yet." Marilyn consoled from outside my stall. "When I was pregnant with my daughter," she continued, "sometime during the first two months, I started bleeding when I was at my son's softball game. I was sure I'd lost her. But, when I went to the doctor, my baby was still there and I have a beautiful two-year-old girl now. Don't give up hope."

That's how Marilyn became my best friend in nursing school.

Sadly, my Ob-Gyn confirmed the news the following Monday. My pregnancy had ended, and I'd lost my future baby. The good news is, I'd been early along enough that I wouldn't need to endure any invasive surgical procedures to remove any fetal material, because there wasn't any that early on.

Thinking getting accepted into nursing school was the hardest part, I was in for a rude awakening.

I had terrible study habits because I had always done so well in college without much trouble. While attending school for my music degree, I would take very detailed notes while in class just as I had in grammar school. Writing down whatever my teachers said helped me remember what was being taught, and a quick review before a test would be all I needed to get a B. Meh, good enough. No one asks you your grades when you graduate. Despite that, I managed to get on the Dean's List when I was pursuing my music degree. Not so much in nursing school, though. Realizing that this technique was not going to work, I found the smartest girls in class, Marilyn being one of them, and made them my best friends.

Distracted and stressed out from my miscarriage, I continued to bleed for a month while trying to absorb all the complicated and terrifying information in nursing school. It was all so foreign and outside of the box compared to my previous artistic and musical education. Holy shit, I had no idea how to retain this information. I might as well have been reading Egyptian Hieroglyphics.

The whole experience of being in nursing school was one long gaslighting head trip. Right before I started nursing school, I met a woman in a yoga class who was a nurse. She had graduated from the same school I was about to start. She said, "Oh, I love being a nurse. But, nursing school? I literally cried every day. It was so hard, I hated it."

And she wasn't the first person to warn me.

I met another nurse at a baby shower right before I started nursing school. She told me, "I love school, and I love being a nurse. But I hated nursing school. It was the worst. It was not like going to college for liberal arts at all. It was absolute torture!"

I wondered, what the heck are they doing to people in nursing school that is making them hate it so much? Well, I soon found out and I've got to be honest, the problems in the medical industry start in the classroom.

"There are no stupid questions" is only true in other areas of education. In nursing school, every single question you ask your instructors is taken to mean that you didn't do your homework. There never seemed to be enough time to study. I was working a mere twelve hours a week at a yoga studio and felt like it was too much. My study habits were already poor, for one. I felt like I needed more time than most. It would take me forever to sit down and focus. I'd incentivize myself to sit and study by keeping a box of cookies next to me and just eating them until they were gone.

My diet pretty much consisted of Dunkin Donuts and Burger King while in nursing school. Those were the two restaurants that were across from the school's clinical lab. A chai latte with a cheese-bread twist and some chocolate munchkins for breakfast. Chicken fingers, fries, and a Dr. Pepper for dinner. And tons of popcorn and Pepperidge Farm Milano cookies when I studied.

The only thing that was keeping me from getting out of shape was that I was working the front desk at a hot yoga studio. I wasn't always able to join the yoga classes while I was on the clock. But mopping the floors and cleaning the studio after class was rigorous enough to keep my figure. I was far from healthy, though.

Nursing school just cemented a lot of my already-bad habits. Such as not planning for meals and eating junk food. And using my debit card until it was declined. And scarfing down entire boxes of Entenmann's donuts while I did my homework.

I was forced to become more focused when studying. I was forced to develop better study habits if I was going to pass. It was always a frenzy in the cafeteria before tests, with nursing students sitting around every table, textbooks open, index cards spread out. Constant background chatter about what will be on the next quiz, students freaking out, causing you to second guess what you thought you knew.

Everyone in my class had been a straight-A (some with an occasional B) student before starting nursing school. Now we were all struggling to get a 74.5 percent, the absolute minimum grade you needed to pass. Once your grade fell below 74.5 percent, you were kicked out. You could repeat whatever semester you received a failing grade in once, but if you failed more than one semester in nursing school, you'd have to start all over again from the beginning. My GPA was literally 0.1 points away from passing: 74.4. I was getting so stressed out I could barely retain anything I was reading.

So I decided to stop going to study groups and try to relax. Instead of going to the cafeteria in the morning before tests, I decided to sleep in, do some yoga in the morning, grab a white chocolate mocha and an egg sandwich from Starbucks, and then show up for the test.

And by taking this approach, I started passing nursing school. I just focused on what I was studying the night before and would let it go the next day. Once I started to calm down, I found myself carving out more time to study. I found myself doing some yoga every day before I studied. After doing yoga, I started noticing I wouldn't want to eat McDonald's. I slowly started creating habits that reduced my stress before I would take a test.

Back in 1983, a study at Georgetown University showed that stress reduces a person's IQ by approximately 13 percent. More recently, it was found that financial stress does exactly the same. When I stopped stressing myself out over things I couldn't control, my grades began to improve, too. My GPA went from a 74.4 to an 86. A 13 percent improvement, coincidentally.

I could not just wing my way through nursing school and expect to pass. I had to learn how to learn. And I had to practice good habits until they became automatic.

Just like learning to ride a motorcycle, nursing school was daunting. At times, terrifying. Out of my comfort zone.

Marilyn was voted as class president, but her vice president failed out of nursing school the first semester. In spite of my protests, Marilyn appointed me to be the class vice president.

This is where our trouble began.

Marilyn and I were asked to monitor a quiz. When our professors left the room, a bunch of girls started Googling the answers on the computer. They didn't even hide the fact that they were cheating, and these were easy questions! For example, what is a normal body temperature? You don't even need to go to nursing school to learn that. So when we collected and handed the quiz papers in, and our teachers asked us if everyone had followed the honor system, we were honest and said, "No, ma'am. Not everyone followed the honor system."

After several students were reprimanded, Marilyn and I were the targets of hate from anyone who thought cheating was okay. As if nursing school wasn't hard enough. We couldn't imagine allowing someone who had cheated their way through nursing school to take care of our loved ones in the future...or even ourselves.

So now we had to deal with cattiness, gossip, and even an investigation by the Dean. Many of our professors boycotted our graduation because the Dean allowed several girls who had cheated to pass. Apparently, someone's mother even threatened a lawsuit.

Nursing school was a whole different animal. It absolutely pushed me to my limit, mentally and physically, and it did pay off. I did learn how to deal with poop and blood. Literally and figuratively. I also learned how to deal with poopy people and bloody liars. Finally, science and algebra weren't mystical challenges anymore.

I used to dread math tests in grammar school. Yet I found myself wanting to do math problems all day long in nursing school. At least there was only one correct answer when it came to math. The rest of the tests in nursing school were multiple choice nightmares with a bit of truth in each of the answers. My brain felt like ground beef after every test. We walked on eggshells around our professors. If someone's cell phone rang during clinicals at the hospital, it was grounds for failure. Marilyn had shut her ringer off, but since she had kids, she'd keep her cell phone in her pocket. One day at clinicals, even after I'd witnessed her silencing her phone, it rang anyway. When the professor shot her a deadly look, Marilyn froze for a second, then literally threw her ringing smart phone in the garbage. Then she stated to our professor without blinking, "I am so fucking serious."

So I got in the habit of leaving my cell phone in my car.

That's where my phone was the day my mother died.

November 2011

I left my phone in my car, as I always did when I was in clinical rotation at the hospital. I'd been assigned to a man who was handcuffed to his hospital bed. He'd been in jail and had faked a seizure in order to get out for a day. I was exhausted when that clinical rotation ended. Once back in my car, I saw that there were several missed calls from Arkansas on my cell phone.

I knew immediately that my mother was gone. I remember feeling completely unaffected when I called the social worker back and she told me my mother had died in her sleep the night before. For me, she had already died a long time ago. Even when we had shopped for wedding dresses together in California, the happy little pixie-ballerina I knew and loved so long ago was no longer with me.

It wasn't until I had a meltdown during a nursing study group that I realized my mother's death was really affecting me. So used to burying my emotions and disassociating from anything in my life that was too difficult, I realized that my mother's death was starting to make all my past trauma back up on me. It took several weeks for all the happy memories of my mom that I had buried deep in my unconscious to resurface. Everything I'd needed to mourn, but couldn't while my mother was still alive, came flooding back. All our trips to the mall, our lunch dates, watching *Little House on the Prairie* after school, going to the fabric store to copy Laura Ingalls Wilder's prairie-style dresses, shopping for Princess Leia *Star Wars* action figures, going to double feature matinees at the theater in town. Trips to the beach in the summer. Getting our hair done together. So many happy memories that I'd buried because they were too hard to relive while my mother was alive.

I spent winter break looking at photos of my mother the way I remembered her. Pictures that had been too painful to look at while she was still alive. A picture of us taken in 1978 in the mountains in the Philippines, sitting on a bench. I'm seven and a half years old, holding a purple and yellow balloon, and leaning against my mother. Another of us taken a few minutes later with me standing on a rock as tall as I am, holding the same balloon. I'm smiling at the camera, while my mother stands in front of me, her head forward, her eyes attempting to look all the way to the right to make sure I'm not falling off the rock. Another picture of my mother smiling at the camera with me by her side, both of us sitting in a patch of grass near my great-uncle's lake house. There is a freshly scraped knee visible under my shorts covered in a Band-Aid. I found all her old ballet photos. I made copies of the photos of my mom looking the way I believed she'd want everyone to remember her, and sent them to the nursing home where she died. I wanted them to know that the stories of how she had been a ballet dancer were true. They hadn't been some weird psychiatric delusions. I wanted them to see that she hadn't been just some dirty homeless woman. She had been someone's wife, mother, sister, and friend. She had dreams like everyone else. She had people who loved her.

I remembered when I was a teenager, my mother mentioned she wanted to be cremated. So that's what I did. She is buried in a town called Mahwah in New Jersey. She always wanted to live in Mahwah, but was never able to.

With my mother's death and my recent miscarriage on my mind, I was barely keeping my head above water. In spite of all this, I somehow managed to tick my GPA up the extra points I needed to continue nursing school. When I started nursing school, I had the worst study habits. But after practicing new habits until they became automatic, I was able to get through nursing school, despite all the stress, loss, and drama going on simultaneously.

In May of 2013, I passed nursing school and became a registered nurse. Thinking about other patients who suffered from mental illness like my mother kept me motivated. People who had such severe mental illness, it was hard for others to eke out any compassion for them whatsoever. I felt like I needed to become the nurse someone like my mother would need. Someone who understands emotional pain. Someone who would not forget that homeless people and those suffering from psychosis are human beings who may have loved ones who are powerless to save them.

Somehow, I didn't fail out of any semesters, or have to repeat any classes. I passed them all, not always with flying colors, but I passed them regardless. And to top it off, I passed the NCLEX licensing exam on the first try too.

It was a miracle, but I learned to transform my poor study habits into good ones, and I became a registered nurse.

I knew there were times when learning to ride my motorcycle was going to be a really tedious process. Like nursing school, learning to ride a motorcycle was completely different than anything else I'd ever done in my life. It was completely and utterly outside of my comfort zone. I was going to have to be focused and committed to the process, just like I had been in nursing school. I was going to have to ask myself, "What are the qualities of a responsible, proficient motorcyclist?" and adopt those qualities.

I decided there were two different kinds of people who rode motorcycles. First, there are the impulsive adrenaline junkies. They are the risk takers without any regard for their safety or anyone else's. Then, there's the gadget geek who loves a challenge and loves the process of learning new things. (And maybe there are riders who fall in between the two. So, okay, three types).

I figured I was more of the latter. I loved looking at all the different kinds of motorcycles. Watching videos of motovloggers on YouTube and learning about motorcycle maintenance became a new pastime. I found a couple of female motovloggers who were short in stature, like me, and enjoyed learning about how they overcame their vertical challenges. I also loved sitting on the back of my husband's motorcycles. I didn't have to be scared because I totally trusted him. I could just enjoy the ride and not worry about a thing, except holding on.

But then there were times I really wanted to go for a ride, but my husband just wasn't up for it. Or there were times when he just needed to go for a ride by himself, and I could respect that. If I wanted to be able to go for a motorcycle ride whenever I wanted to, I was going to have to learn how to ride on my own. There were things I could practice when I was off the motorcycle, I realized, that would improve my riding skills on the motorcycle. It started with changing my habits when driving my car. Which led to noticing that I was being more mindful in my car.

Which led me to become more mindful in my life in general.

Then I started telling myself to stop reacting to things when I was on the motorcycle. Instead, I tried to respond to situations. It took me quite a few days to get over the emotional trauma of grinding my motorcycle into the asphalt, so I started building a "response." I'd sit on the bike in my garage with the engine off, working on pulling in the front brake with one finger while avoiding opening up the throttle.

Sometimes, my mind would go back to my old thinking patterns and I'd get frustrated when I'd believe I should be further along with my skills. Who am I competing with? I'm not in a race. I'm just trying to learn how to ride a motorcycle. As a full-time nurse during a pandemic, I had limited time to practice as much as I wanted to. And I needed to respect that. I was determined to learn how to ride, so I was going to have to have patience.

I told myself that it didn't matter if it took me a year before I felt like I could go out on a public road by myself. I had to respect my own personal learning process. I promised myself I would perfect all my slow skills before going out on the road by myself. Eventually, I found myself enjoying perfecting all the little skills. I'd make videos and post them on YouTube. In fact, some of my most popular videos are the ones where I'm not actually riding, but demonstrating how to stop with one foot down or how to pick up the motorcycle when it is three times your weight. When I started to love the process, things started falling into place.

It's easy to think of Zen as a goal or destination. But it's really something that is right in our reach right now. When you are truly just living with clarity in each moment, then life stops feeling like a to-do list, or a series of checklists. Life stops feeling like you are waiting to reach some destination in order to allow yourself to be happy.

Zen is the most difficult, yet easiest thing to do.

10

ZEN MOTORCYCLE HABIT #10
ENJOY THE RIDE

"Sometimes it's a little better to travel than to arrive."

—ROBERT M. PIRSIG, *ZEN AND THE ART OF MOTORCYCLE MAINTENANCE*

How I learned from the past and prepared for the future so I could live in the present

In 1994, in the early hours of my birthday, June 6, my best friend, Ted, became my boyfriend. We had been sitting on the couch watching *Ren and Stimpy*. Or maybe it was *Beavis and Butthead*. We started falling asleep and slumping over on each other. I don't know who started it, but the next thing I knew, we were kissing at 4 a.m. When I realized it was 4 a.m, and officially my birthday, I wanted to get home before the sun came up and my dad started asking questions. So I ran out of there as fast as I could.

The next day, I was anxious and freaking out. I needed Ted to be my friend, but I would get so paranoid and insecure if I was in a relationship, I ultimately would just sabotage it. I didn't want that to happen with Ted. I needed advice, so I talked on the phone with my girlfriends for hours and hours and hours the next day. What to say to Ted, how to say it, and how to tell him we should just be friends.

As the average person did not own a cell phone in 1994, I had to call Ted at the gas station where he worked. One of the guys in the repair shop picked up, and I could hear a mocking, sing-songy tone in his voice, "Tehhhhh-ed! Leslie is on the phone!"

"Happy birthday," Ted said. "Can you come over tonight so I can give you your birthday presents?"

Perfect. I could go over there and tell him I was half asleep and didn't know what I was doing when we started making out, but I can't afford to lose him as a friend. I rehearsed my speech over and over in my head the entire drive over there. I was sure of exactly what I was going to say.

Ted answered the door when I got there. He had presents in his hands and a card. The card read, "Thanks for giving us a chance to be more than friends. You are my best friend and I really care about you a lot."

After reading that, there was no way I could break up with him right now. "Well," I figured, "I could always break up with him some other day."

Ted had bought me a bunch of little gifts, all of which I loved. He bought me this plaid flannel shirt I had been eyeing. And a little black choker necklace with one turquoise, one bright pink, and one silver bead on it, with a teardrop-shaped peace sign dangling from the middle.

He also bought me a little white T-shirt with a picture of Felix the Cat on it. He and his mother served me lemon and vanilla buttercream cake. They lit some candles, and sang happy birthday to me.

October 1992

Two years before we started dating, Ted and I were good friends. I had met him through my college friend Heidi. Heidi and I loved music, dogs, and going for hikes. Like my cousins Vivian and Margarita, Heidi was as adventurous as a Bond Girl. She drove across the country and camped by herself several times. She rode a motorcycle. She and Ted had become friends due to their love of off-roading in their big old trucks. Ted and I became best buddies pretty quickly, and were on the phone, watching movies, or meeting up at a diner regularly. Heidi and Ted were friends with my ex-boyfriend, Cyrus.

I was obsessed with Cyrus. Cyrus and I were both twenty when we met during a jazz concert in the college auditorium that was mandatory for all music majors to attend. He played the guitar, loved classic rock, blues, and jazz, and had long hair that hung in brown ringlets around his pale-blue Neptunian eyes. He was the first guy who ever told me he loved me. So, of course, I had to break up with him. That was just too scary. A few weeks after he told me he was falling in love with me, I convinced myself that he was bored with me and I broke up with him. And even though I was the one who broke up with him, I was heartbroken, devastated, crushed. I'd blather on and on about him to whoever would listen.

The night I met Ted, Heidi had made plans for all three of us, plus my old friend Liz from high school, to go to Hoboken for drinks. But Heidi was asked to stay late at work. So she gave Ted my phone number and told him to call me to let me know that she couldn't make it.

Ted's voice on my 1990s answering machine said, "Hi. This is Heidi's friend, Ted. She wanted me to call you because she can't make it out with us tonight. But, if you still want to meet up with me and Liz, let me know. I think our friend Joey might come too."

When I heard his voice, I thought to myself "I wonder if I'm going to meet my future husband tonight?"

Ted and I met up in Big Jim's Pizza's parking lot. My first thought was, "He's probably not my future husband." He was about twice as tall as I was and there didn't seem to be a romantic vibe between us. We took my car to the train station and met up with Liz and Joey. The four of us ended up taking the PATH train to the Village in Manhattan.

We were drinking margaritas at a bar near Bleecker Street and chit chatting, when I found out that Ted went to grammar school with Cyrus, and that they had been good friends. Naturally, this was my cue to start talking incessantly about (and pining away for) Cyrus non-stop.

Ted listened intently. Nodding his head. Telling me he understood how I felt. Interjecting a compassionate sigh at all the right moments. He told me he recently broke up with his girlfriend, too. He was feeling sad about it. I'm sure he wanted to talk about what he was going through, too. But I didn't let him get a word in edgewise. I just kept going on and on about Cyrus.

At one point, Ted said, "Wow, you are, like, obsessed with Cyrus."

I sat there for a moment, then blurted out, "Oh my god. I am. I hate myself."

I started crying.

"I was just joking." Ted tried to make light of it, but I knew he was right, and I was embarrassed.

I was totally obsessed with Cyrus, and everyone knew it.

"No, it's true. I am! What's wrong with me?" I cried.

It was pathetic.

I wished there was some kind of surgical procedure to remove the memories of Cyrus from my brain. "A Cyrus lobotomy," Ted joked.

Liz and Joey were saying, "What the hell, Ted? Why is she crying?"

"It's not his fault. I'm too embarrassed to tell you why I'm crying," I said.

Ted called me the next day to tell me he felt bad. He was sorry for making fun of me. He said that he was having a tough time not thinking about his ex, too.

"You can call me anytime if you need to talk. I understand."

"Really?"

"Sure, you can talk to me."

I took that literally. I called Ted anytime I felt upset about Cyrus. Which was pretty much all the time.

What time was it? Eight o'clock in the morning while Ted was at work at the gas station? I'd call him and cry about Cyrus. Four o'clock in the morning and only two hours before Ted had to get up for work? I'd call him and pine over Cyrus.

After a few months of these late-night talks on the landline, our parents were getting annoyed. When we were talking on the phone, it would wake up everyone in the household.

"Can't you wait until the morning to talk?" Ted's mother pleaded with him one night when we were gabbing away at two a.m.

So, in order to allow his mom to sleep, Ted would come over to my dad's condo to keep me company in the middle of the night. Or we'd meet up at one of the thousands of 24-hour New Jersey diners that were open. We'd eat extra crispy French fries slathered in melted mozzarella cheese and drink Cokes. Whenever I'd be upset about some boy I had a crush on, I'd call Ted.

One of my good friends from high school was getting married. Since I didn't have an official boyfriend, she didn't let me bring a "plus-one" in the interest of saving money on the reception. Otherwise, I probably would've brought Ted with me. Ted had actually helped me pick out the dress I was going to wear to her autumn wedding: a 1990s goth-y dark-red crushed velvet long sheath with a black choker necklace and platform heels.

So this friend that was getting married, her brother had been the first guy I had consensual sex with four years earlier. Trey. Yes, the same Trey I would someday be engaged to.

End of Summer, New Jersey, 1988

Towards the end of the summer after I graduated from high school (and after Jimmy in the orange Beetle had dumped me), Trey and I had secretly started fooling around with each other. It happened after a BBQ at a mutual friend's house. We were all hanging out in the backyard, and Trey started yawning and stretching and saying he was getting tired and wanted to head home soon. Every time his sister offered to drive him home, he'd say, "Nah, I'll hang out for a bit longer."

So, as an experiment, I told myself the next time Trey yawned and stretched, I'd offer him a ride home and see what happened. Sure enough, he was like, "Oh, yeah, if you could drive me home, Leslie, that would be great."

When we got in my car, Trey said, "So, I really don't want to go home. I have a joint and thought we could smoke it together?"

I pulled over into the parking lot of a strip mall that was closed and we lit up the joint. After it was my turn to take a hit of weed, we started fooling around.

This type of thing would go on for the next two summers and whenever Trey was home from college on a break. He didn't have his own car but shared an old Dodge station wagon with his sister when he was in town. We'd all be at a party; he'd pretend to be tired. His sister would offer to drive him home, he'd say no. So I'd offer to drive him home, then we'd find somewhere to park and make out and do basically everything but have sex.

One summer weekend when my father was (as usual) out

of town (with his girlfriend), Trey called me in the middle of the night, and I drove over and picked him up so we could fool around at my place. Just before the sun came up, I drove him home before his sister and parents woke up. On more than one occasion, I had just finished dropping Trey off at home, driven back to my house, put my head on the pillow, and his sister would call me and say, "Hey, what are you doing? I'm coming over and picking you up so we can go down the shore! Be ready in twenty minutes!"

January 1990

Two years after we started our secret affair, I was nearing my twentieth birthday. Trey was home from college for winter break. He called me up one chilly day in January and invited me over for pizza and beer. I decided on my way over to his house that this was it. I was going to have consensual sex for the first time and Trey was going to do the job. My birthday was five months away, and I was NOT going to go into my twenties a virgin. Even though I'd been raped by Dan several months earlier, I still considered myself a virgin. That wasn't sex, it had been an assault.

Trey and I ate the pizza and pounded the Heinekens. We were fooling around all over his parents' house. On the couch, in the kitchen, the laundry room, his room, his sister's room. The grand finale happened in his parents' bed, missionary style. Afterwards, I looked at my eyes in the mirror to see if I noticed any difference. One of my Catholic high school teachers who was also a nun would always say that you could tell when a woman wasn't a virgin anymore, because the innocence in her eyes was gone. I thought maybe I'd never had any innocence in my eyes to begin with.

Trey graduated from college the following summer and I hoped and prayed maybe he would be my boyfriend now that he wasn't living three states away. Instead, he got a job offer to be the manager of a swanky restaurant in Los Angeles. He moved to California, on the other side of the country, and didn't bother contacting me again, which left me feeling discarded and devastated.

September 1993

Seeing Trey for the first time in three years at the wedding made me realize I still was into him. So, of course, after my friend's wedding, Trey and I got drunk at a bar next to the reception hall with the rest of the wedding party and the new bride and groom. He started yawning and stretching and saying he was tired. So I offered to give him a ride back to the hotel. Instead, we went back to my place.

In the middle of us having sex, my phone rang and his sister left a message on my answering machine in an irritated voice: "Leslie. Is Trey with you again? I thought you were driving him back to the hotel, but we can't find him. Can you please drive him back to the hotel when you guys are done? He's supposed to take our grandmother to the airport in the morning."

I felt like shit afterwards because he was going back to California in two days, and I knew I was going to be forgotten again. And I also felt like shit for upsetting my friend on her wedding night.

I had no idea that six years after my friend's wedding, I would move to Los Angeles to pursue music, and he would be one of the few people I'd know there. And that I would end up getting engaged to him.

But I didn't know that at the time, and like I said, I was already starting to feel like shit. I dropped Trey back off at the Marriott, then drove home and did what I usually would do when I was upset about some guy. I called Ted at 3 a.m. and started whining about it.

I heard his mother in the background. "It is 3 a.m., Ted. Can't this wait until tomorrow?"

"Um, I'm just going to come to your house," Ted told me.

As usual, I cried. Then we talked for a little bit, and then he fell asleep on the rug of my bedroom floor. He did this all the time, never hinting at wanting a romantic relationship with me. At the time, my girlfriends advised me that I should give Ted the "I just want to be friends" speech. They'd tell me that it seemed like I was leading him on, hanging out with him all hours of the night. So, on their advice, I told Ted I just wanted to be friends and hoped he never felt that I was leading him on.

To which he responded, "Uh, okay. Are you conceited or did I hit on you without realizing it? No offense, but all you do is cry over other guys, and I don't find that attractive."

I laughed, "Ah, Liz and Heidi insisted I make sure you knew we were just friends. I told them it wasn't like that and that you only thought of me as a friend!"

And we were best friends. Genuinely best friends.

June 1994

That is, until two years later when we started dating, on that couch, watching *Ren and Stimpy* or *Beavis and Butthead* at 4 a.m. on my twenty-fourth birthday. He was the only guy I ever dated that I wasn't addicted to. Back then, I still didn't know what a healthy relationship looked like. I confused codependency for passion. What I thought was passionate, soulmate love, was actually an anxiety attack over an obsession. If I didn't feel this way about someone, I took it to mean there was no spark or passion.

But, when I was with Ted, I wasn't worried. I felt safe and grounded. I didn't feel like I was going to have an anxiety attack every time I thought about our relationship. I didn't feel like I had to break up with him before he broke up with me. Ted and I dated pretty seriously for a few years.

Yet I still wasn't ready to make a commitment to him. I felt like if I didn't get out of New Jersey before the year 2000, I would never get out of New Jersey. I love New Jersey. It's just that everything about it pisses me off, and I needed to get out of there and go on my own journey before I could share my journey with anyone else.

June 1999

Born and raised in Bergen County, New Jersey, I finally left my home state for California in 1999. When I was a toddler, we lived in a high rise across the Hudson River in Fort Lee with views of the Manhattan skyline. Then we moved to the suburbs, where I grew up surrounded by kids my age. It was definitely a privileged life, living in upper middle class white suburbia. Even though I looked more Filipino as a child than I do now, I recognize that I grew up with white privilege.

Living with my father up until my late twenties, I just couldn't justify moving out and paying rent in New Jersey when I had a free place to live there. I didn't want to be living with my father at age thirty, though. So, if I was going to move out, then I was *really* going to move out. Accustomed to being in such close proximity to Manhattan, I wanted to live near an entertainment hub.

I'd broken up with Ted a couple years earlier. I wasn't ready to give up on pursuing my dreams of being a singer yet. And I certainly wasn't ready for marriage. Not wanting to commit to anyone before having a chance at living my life out on my own, it was time for me to go.

Los Angeles, California was going to be my new home. I'd chosen L.A. because it was practically the entertainment center of the universe, and I wanted to take one more shot at a singing career before I turned thirty. Plus the weather in

L.A. was nearly perfect every single day. I could live near the beach and keep my car. It would be a dream come true. So I had a big garage sale in my friend Kris's driveway and sold a bunch of my stuff. Then, a few days later, I packed up my car with Kris in tow. The last week of June, we started a ten-day journey across the country from New Jersey to Los Angeles.

My first apartment out on my own was a studio in West Los Angeles. It was about a mile from UCLA and a ten-minute drive to Venice Beach. The kitchen had brand-new Mexican tiles on the counter. There was a pool outside of my big glass windows. It was right near the intersection of the 10 and 405 freeways. Whenever a truck would take the exit from the 10 to the 405 south, I would wonder if we were having an earthquake.

In the mornings before going to work, I would drive to Venice Beach and roller skate for an hour. There was always a man with a long white beard taking a morning seaside walk on the beach. He looked like Santa Claus, except he was practically naked, only wearing a red G-string. The surprising thing was how no one in Venice found it surprising.

In the evenings, I'd sit under a palm tree and write in my journal while watching surfers surf into the sunset. Chills ran down my spine whenever I'd look up at a palm tree. I'd think, "I did it all by myself. I moved out of my father's house and got my own apartment. All the way in California."

I spent ten years in Los Angeles.

I did call Ted once about five years after I'd moved there. I thought maybe enough time had passed. Maybe we could be friends again. His mother answered the phone, and she told me he had a girlfriend and they were out together, but she'd give him the message. He didn't call me back. I understood why, and I didn't hold it against him. But I'd regretted that we didn't stay friends after we broke up. I had handled it all wrong because I hadn't been ready.

March 2009

Just four months shy of my ten-year anniversary of moving to Los Angeles, I felt like it was time to go back to New Jersey. Still single and band-less, I was starting to feel like the party was over and it was time to leave. I was working in the back office at a desk in the dispensary. The desktop wasn't a straight rectangle. Instead, the edges had a wavy shape to them and they made me think of Ted riding his motorcycle on the twisty roads around Greenwood Lake. I thought how he had been the best boyfriend I ever had. I had just been too stupid to realize it a decade earlier. I figured he was probably married with kids by now.

Ted and I had a real relationship. It had been based on a real friendship. It hadn't been codependent. We never had drunken bootie calls. I never needed a "fix" from Ted. He just wanted to love me. So I just sat there thinking I'd blown the only real relationship I'd ever been in.

And then one day, the unexpected happened. About two months before I was planning to leave Los Angeles, I got a message through my Facebook page while I was at work. It was from Ted.

He said, "Hi there. How are you? I know it's been a long time. I got your message seven years ago that you called, but I couldn't call you back at the time. I hope you don't hold it against me. I thought it would be nice to talk to an old friend. You really were my best friend. Hope to hear from you. Take care. Ted."

At first I freaked out. Was this some kind of a joke? I had just been thinking about him a few days earlier. I thought I was being punk'd. When I calmed down, I wrote him back and we scheduled a time to talk on the phone later that night. Coincidentally, when I got home from work that evening, the divorce papers ending my green card marriage were in the mailbox. Tiago and I were officially no longer married.

And I didn't think that was a coincidence.

Ted and I talked on the phone that night until it was midnight Pacific Time and 3 a.m. Eastern Time. I told him I was moving back to New Jersey in about two months. I was going to go to nursing school. He said he missed me. He could help me with my chemistry class. He would teach me algebra. He said he still had his 1993 Suzuki GSX-R and we could ride around on it all summer when I moved back.

Then he said, "I have something to tell you. I love you."

∾

The day I flew back to New Jersey, I got to my dad's house and unpacked all my things in the bedroom he had set up for me. Later, Ted picked me up and we hit a diner on Route 17 in Paramus for old time's sake. The next night, I went over to Ted's apartment to hang out. But I never left.

"Does this mean we are officially back together?" Ted asked me.

January 14, 2011

Two years later, Ted and I got married on a snowy day in January in front of a big old fireplace at a historic tavern where George Washington himself had once slept. Sherri was my maid of honor. Greg, Ted's old roommate who let me ride his YSR motorcycle, was our best man. During his speech, he talked about the time he and Ted tried to teach me to ride when we were younger. Sherri (my college roommate) Heidi (who had introduced me to Ted back in college), and Danielle (who I'd lived with in the haunted house in East L.A.) were also in my wedding.

My journey back to myself was long and challenging.

But it made me who I am today. I couldn't take the shortcut on this journey with Ted. I had too much to learn on my own. I needed to learn what real love was before we could join our paths.

I didn't know what real love was then, but I understood now.

July 2020

Ted and I were getting ready to embark on a trip we'd been dreaming about for years. When Ted and I started dating in 1994, we spent a lot of time talking about how great it would be to take a trip on a Harley Davidson up the coast of California. We wanted to camp along the way. And it only took about twenty-six years to make that dream come true. Well, almost come true.

Ted finally bought that Harley Davidson he'd been dreaming about not too long after his fiftieth birthday. The first time we went for a ride, as I was hopping onto the back, I was nervous as heck. I was thinking how happy I was that I wasn't the one "driving" the damn thing.

We took a ride through Hermosa and Redondo Beaches. Then we drove through the winding streets on the cliffs over the ocean of Palos Verdes. The sun was setting and the sky was glowing orange, yellow, and violet, like rainbow sorbet. Catalina Island was in view off the coast. It was so beautiful, I literally got tears in my eyes on that ride.

When we got home, I was so disappointed the ride was over. I wanted to get back on the motorcycle so badly. The next morning, I told my husband that I wanted to try to learn how to ride a motorcycle again.

He was annoyed. "Seriously? We just moved from a rural town in New Jersey where it would be perfect to learn how to ride. There is too much traffic here in Los Angeles. Too many tourists on the road. This is a dangerous city to want to learn to ride a motorcycle in."

I secretly started scheming how I could learn to ride without him, googling MSF courses on the internet.

A few hours later, he came back and said, "Okay, if you want to learn to ride, we need to do it the right way, unlike the first time I tried to teach you. You need to be on a dirt-bike for at least a year. You need to do all the wiping out and crashing and make all your mistakes in the dirt as far away from traffic as possible."

So I scoured Craigslist. And then I found the perfect little Kawasaki KX 85, and my motorcycle journey began. I just needed to wait until it wasn't 110 degrees out in the desert so I could ride it. Every summer in California seemed to get hotter and hotter as the years went by. The fires seemed to be getting bigger and bigger.

When I first moved to California in the 1990s, I remembered hearing about one or two fires within a decade. And they usually happened at the same time of the year. Nowadays, there will be four or five fires burning simultaneously. There is no more fire season, as they seem to be breaking out all year round now.

The summer Ted and I planned our road trip on the Harley, the entire coast caught on fire. San Jose and Santa Cruz were evacuated due to fires. Big Sur was closed. Ventura and Ojai were burning up as well. The fires forced us into cancelling our motorcycle trip. Instead, we took our labradoodle to the dog beaches in San Diego, and planned a lunch with my cousin Margarita. Since I had already taken ten days off work for vacation, I also decided to sign up for the three-day Motorcycle Safety Foundation (MSF) course. When we met up with Margarita for lunch in San Diego, she was so happy to hear I was going to be taking the MSF course and joining the "Filipino cousins' James Bond Girl Motorcycle Riders Club" with her and Vivian.

Wildfires continued to plague California in the summer of 2020. The MSF course I took was in Long Beach, at least sixty miles away from the nearest wildfire. Yet even sixty miles away from the nearest fire, the sky was grey from the smoke. It blocked out the sun. The entire three days of the MSF class, it rained ashes from the sky. This inspired me to choose a different kind of motorcycle. When I started my journey to learn to ride, getting an electric motorcycle was not even on my radar. But, after riding the emissions-free Zero Electric during the course, I was sold.

My journey didn't always go as planned. But that doesn't mean that it wasn't amazing.

I didn't end up in life exactly where I thought I would. I didn't become a famous singer. I was never able to have children. I am not a rich billionaire. Yet I'd wasted months, years, maybe even decades waiting for these things to happen so that I could finally allow myself to be happy.

That's why we have to remember to be present where we are, wherever we are. We don't always end up where we think we will on our journey, but if we don't learn to enjoy the journey, our lives will just pass us by. Maybe joy isn't the appropriate emotion for every situation in life. Maybe every ride isn't the most fun ride. Some rides don't go as planned. Some rides may not be enjoyable at all. Other rides are so beautiful; everything just falls into place, and it practically brings tears to one's eyes. Sometimes, things turn out better than planned.

We can respect every moment of our lives by being present for them. Good or bad, just keep staying present in those moments. Every moment on your journey is your life. Make sure you're living in it.

September 2021

The first time I went on a real motorcycle ride on a public road alongside my husband, I was shocked at how easy and comfortable everything felt. Spending hours in my garage building muscle memory on the motorcycle with the engine off, practicing picking up my motorcycle in the driveway, the eight months I'd spent weaving in and out of cones in a parking lot. It had magically paid off. So many times, I'd felt frustrated. So many times, I'd felt like I wasn't improving at all. I'd even thought about selling my motorcycle at one point because I felt like I was wasting my time. Yet I kept at it.

It.All.Paid.Off.

No longer on the back of Ted's Harley, I rode my own motorcycle through the same beautiful twisty roads on the cliffs of Palos Verdes overlooking the Pacific Ocean. The same roads that I'd ridden through on the back of my husband's Harley a year earlier. Now riding my own motorcycle, I'd been rewarded by embracing the process of learning to ride, respecting my boundaries, remaining patient with myself, and cultivating skills that turned into good riding habits. I did not experience any anxiety, panic, or fear whatsoever on that first ride. I was 100 percent in the moment, focused on what I was doing.

I had finally learned to trust myself, and that was one of the greatest gifts my motorcycle had taught me.

I was finally riding my motorcycle on my own. I had earned the Zen state of mind I found myself in.

That is how you practice Zen.

AFTERWORD

As I was writing this book, some amazing things happened. I was ready to tell my full truth. I was ready to own my life, the good, the bad, the ugly. However, I didn't expect friends, family members, and ex-boyfriends of mine to be okay with me exposing their stories while I was telling mine. I didn't want to disrespect anyone else's privacy as I told my own story. Everyone I was able to contact before finishing this book gave me their blessings to tell my truth. The full truth. I had no idea how therapeutic writing this story would be. I found myself healing from old wounds and scars so deep, I hadn't even realized how much these old wounds were still affecting me.

While I was in the middle of writing this book, I was diagnosed on the autism spectrum. Looking at the stories in retrospect, it is so clear to me how my misdiagnoses and underlying ASD had contributed to my codependent behavior. I realize that the story of women on the spectrum, such as myself, deserves its own book, and that will be my next venture.

Writing this book put me on the most amazing spiritual healing journey. I came to know myself better. The panic and anxiety that used to render me helpless like a deer in headlights became something I'd notice and manage before it took its grip. The greatest gift I received from writing this, is realizing how much love and support I've had on my journey. So many people have helped me when I was struggling. They loved me at my best. They loved me at my worst. I owe them all my sincerest and most humble gratitude. My family, friends, and lovers have made me who I am today. They are part of my story now, and I'm so grateful for that.

ACKNOWLEDGEMENTS

Special thanks to these individuals, friends, and family members. This book would not be what it is without you. Sherri Gauthier: Thank you for encouraging me during the early stages of this book. Tawny Sverdlin MLIS: This book would not be nearly as good as it is without your creative direction. "Diva" Danielle White: Thank you for encouraging me to add some of the raw stories you lived through with me. Jen Sincero: Thank you for always supporting me, encouraging me, and believing in me as a writer.

Margarita, Vivian, Mary Ellen, and Maria Victoria Reyes: The Filipino Cousins, "Bond Girls" Forever. Ronni Lynn Cramer: The sister I always wanted. Craig T.: One Love, my big brother. Heidi: the other Bond Girl. Kris: Thank you for the cross-country adventure. My dad, My Uncle Pete, Aunt Hannelore, Cousin Michael, Uncle Cesar, Aunt Tita: The Reyes clan, my Filipino Family.

Ted Waddington: my husband, my best friend, my protection, my love.

Janet, Kristen, and Kim Raimann: My extended family. Rosa Ramos, nursing hero and veteran: thanks for believing in me. John Michael Montgomery: I can tell that you're still watching over me. Mary Withers: my rave mama. Suzi and Chris, Darren Linder, The Craw, and Marcela Joy: my Portland family. Marilyn and Marilyn and Natasha: you helped get me through nursing school alive. Zhanine Robie: for living through the "Matty" saga with me. Carole Pearson:

Dawgsquad mom. Baxter and Luna. Susan S., Inna C., "Big Chris", and Terry Butera For helping me become the best addiction nurse I could.

Crystal B. and Jackie Slevin: Astrologers extraordinaire. Amy White: Yoga Goddess. Jen Celestin: Reiki Master. Dr. Marianne Bays: my favorite Jersey Girl. Alice O'Leary: You are an amazing healer and activist. Jacqueline Patterson: You are an amazing queen. Marcie, Heather, Mary Lynn Mathre, and Eileen Konieczny: Everyone deserves a nurse (ACNA). Shaye H., Bill L., Irene, Heather, Mike M., JoAnna L., and "Dr. Phill" S.: my dispensary family who saved me from a dark time. Lori D., Gio C., Todd S., Andy H., Dan M., and so many others: for helping me survive Los Angeles in the late 2000s. My Uncle Rob, for helping me when I moved back in the late 2010s.

Clutch Motorcycle School in Long Beach, California: for letting me go at my own pace and putting me on a Zero. Hollywood Electrics in West Hollywood: for getting my motorcycle as low as it would go. Zero Motorcycles: for making these awesome electric motorcycles. Gary McDaniel El Sat: The pink weenies. Marcus Murphy: for taking me on your mini-bike in first grade. Magic Toaster: for encouraging me on YouTube. Caroline, aka "Doodle on a Motorcycle" for inspiring me to keep going, and for putting me in your 2022 Calendar. The Litas, Chic Riot, Meghan Stark and Jess "Her Two Wheels", Ann Wilson, Debbie Harry, Pat Benatar, and Susanna Hoffs: for showing me that women can ride and jam just as great as the best of the boys.

And for my Mom: I'll always remember you as my pixie-ballerina, exactly the way you'd want me to.

RESOURCES

Here are some tools to help you on your own healing journey.

Everyone's journey looks different. Some tools work better for certain people than for others.

Some people have found healing by getting involved in churches. Some people find churches traumatizing.

Some people have found healing in medications. Some people feel worse on medications.

Some have found healing in meditation. Some have needed to meet with a psychiatrist or therapist. Others have found group therapy helpful.

Astrology, camping, meditation, medication, hiking, music, dog or cat rescue, medical missions, travel, therapy, psychiatry, yoga…whatever it is that helps you find your path, keep trying. Just don't give up.

I can't tell you what will work for you. But here are some resources to get you started.

Practicing Zen, Where to Start?

The Zen Studies Society
A Buddhist community dedicated to realizing and actualizing our true nature.

https://zenstudies.org/

The Zen Institute of New Zealand
One of the West's most respected Zen training organizations.

http://www.zen.org.nz

Mental Health Resources

NIH, National Center for Complimentary and Integrative Medicine
Some research suggests that meditation may physically change the brain and body and could potentially help to improve many health problems and promote healthy behaviors.

https://www.nccih.nih.gov/health/meditation-in-depth

- Meditation

The National Institute of Mental Health (NIMH)
The leading federal agency for research on mental disorders.

https://www.nimh.nih.gov/

- Schizophrenia
- Depression
- Anxiety
- Bipolar Disorder
- Borderline Personality Disorder

The U.S. Department of Health and Human Services (HHS)

Mission: To enhance the health and well-being of all Americans, by providing for effective health and human services and by fostering sound, sustained advances in the sciences underlying medicine, public health, and social services.

https://www.hhs.gov/programs/topic-sites/autism/index.html

- Adult Autism
- Pre-Menstrual Dysphoric Disorder
- ADHD, OCD

Substance Abuse and Mental Health Services Administration (SAMHSA)

SAMHSA's National Helpline is a free, confidential, 24/7, 365-day-a-year treatment referral and information service (in English and Spanish) for individuals and families facing mental and/or substance use disorders.

SAMHSA's National Helpline: 1-800-662-HELP (4357)

https://www.samhsa.gov/

- Addiction
- Chemical Dependency
- Substance Abuse
- Suicide Prevention

American Foundation for Suicide Prevention (AFSP)
We can all help prevent suicide. The Lifeline provides 24/7, free and confidential support for people in distress.

Suicide Prevention Hotline: 1-800-273-8255 CHAT

- Suicide Prevention Hotline
- Suicide survivors
- Also supports friends and family members who lost loved one to suicide

Motorcycle Resources

Motorcycle Safety Foundation (MSF)
A national, not-for-profit organization promoting the safety of motorcyclists with programs in rider training, operator licensing, and public information. The MSF is sponsored by the U.S. manufacturers and distributors of BMW, BRP, Harley-Davidson, Honda, Indian Motorcycle, Kawasaki, KTM, Suzuki, Triumph, and Yamaha.

https://www.MSF-USA.org

- Motorcycle safety training
- Motorcycle license training
- Beginner and advanced training

The Litas
An international collective for moto-curious and moto-obsessed women.

https://thelitas.co/

MORE FOR READERS

Book Club Guide:
LeslieReyesAuthor.com/bookclubs

Free Printable Poster:
The Ten Zen Principles of Good Motorcycle Riding Habits
LeslieReyesAuthor.com/poster

Subscribe to My Newsletter:
LeslieReyesAuthor.com

ABOUT THE AUTHOR

Leslie Reyes, BSN, RN, is a psychiatric and chemical dependency nurse, yoga teacher, and motorcycle enthusiast.

She has seen mental illness up close, first as the daughter of a schizophrenic mother and later through her own personal mental health struggles. She never expected a motorcycle would one day be the guru she needed to change her life habits and finally learn to trust herself.

Leslie lives with her husband, their five motorcycles, and two dogs in Los Angeles, California. She currently rides a 2021 Zero S electric motorcycle and a 2017 Kawasaki KX-85 dirt bike.

TheZenofLearningtoRideaMotorcycle.com

facebook.com/LolaLeslie66Moto

instagram.com/LolaLeslie66

youtube.com/LolaLeslie66